React Router Qu

Routing in React applications made easy

Sagar Ganatra

BIRMINGHAM - MUMBAI

Copyright and Credits

React Router Quick Start Guide

Copyright © 2018 Packt Publishing

All rights reserved. No part of this book may be reproduced, stored in a retrieval system, or transmitted in any form or by any means, without the prior written permission of the publisher, except in the case of brief quotations embedded in critical articles or reviews.

Every effort has been made in the preparation of this book to ensure the accuracy of the information presented. However, the information contained in this book is sold without warranty, either express or implied. Neither the author(s), nor Packt Publishing or its dealers and distributors, will be held liable for any damages caused or alleged to have been caused directly or indirectly by this book.

Packt Publishing has endeavored to provide trademark information about all of the companies and products mentioned in this book by the appropriate use of capitals. However, Packt Publishing cannot guarantee the accuracy of this information.

Commissioning Editor: Amaraba banerjee
Acquisition Editor: Noyonika Das
Content Development Editor: Kirk Dsouza
Technical Editor: Sushmeeta Jena
Copy Editor: Safis Editing
Project Coordinator: Hardik Bhinde
Proofreader: Safis Editing
Indexer: Mariammal Chettiyar
Graphics: Alishon Mendonsa
Production Coordinator: Shraddha Falebhai

First published: September 2018

Production reference: 1280918

Published by Packt Publishing Ltd.
Livery Place
35 Livery Street
Birmingham
B3 2PB, UK.

ISBN 978-1-78953-255-5

www.packtpub.com

mapt.io

Mapt is an online digital library that gives you full access to over 5,000 books and videos, as well as industry leading tools to help you plan your personal development and advance your career. For more information, please visit our website.

Why subscribe?

- Spend less time learning and more time coding with practical eBooks and Videos from over 4,000 industry professionals
- Improve your learning with Skill Plans built especially for you
- Get a free eBook or video every month
- Mapt is fully searchable
- Copy and paste, print, and bookmark content

packt.com

Did you know that Packt offers eBook versions of every book published, with PDF and ePub files available? You can upgrade to the eBook version at www.packt.com and as a print book customer, you are entitled to a discount on the eBook copy. Get in touch with us at customercare@packtpub.com for more details.

At www.packt.com, you can also read a collection of free technical articles, sign up for a range of free newsletters, and receive exclusive discounts and offers on Packt books and eBooks.

Contributors

About the author

Sagar Ganatra is a frontend engineer and an architect from Bangalore, India. He has more than a decade of experience in developing web and mobile applications. He specializes in architecting projects using JavaScript and frameworks such as React, Angular, and Node. His previous books include *Kendo UI Cookbook* and *Instant Kendo UI Mobile*, both published by Packt Publishing. He also writes about frontend technologies in his blog, *sagarganatra (dot) com*.

About the reviewer

Tadas Subonis started coding roughly when he was thirteen. Since then, he has programmed with PHP, JavaScript, Python, C++, and Java (the language in which he has probably written the most code). He has an MSc in Artificial Intelligence, is a certified professional and a technical lead that has deployed multiple complex projects that were based on web technologies. Also, he is an author of *Reactive Android Programming*.

Mario Krajacic a self-taught JavaScript developer who fell in love with coding while trying to automate tasks at his previous network and projects administrator positions. He is passionate about technology and continuous learning.

Most of his experience comes from working with Node.js and React.js and a major part of his learning journey being Chingu.io—a global collaboration platform for tech-learners.

> I would like to thank the author for writing this book and trusting me with the review and Chance McAllister for a review recommendation and for founding and leading the amazing Chingu community!

Packt is searching for authors like you

If you're interested in becoming an author for Packt, please visit `authors.packtpub.com` and apply today. We have worked with thousands of developers and tech professionals, just like you, to help them share their insight with the global tech community. You can make a general application, apply for a specific hot topic that we are recruiting an author for, or submit your own idea.

Table of Contents

Preface	1
Chapter 1: Introduction to React Router 4 and Creating Your First Route	7
A brief look at React	8
Component-based architecture in React	9
Creating a React component	10
Introduction to React-Router	12
Getting started with React-Router	14
Adding the React-Router library	16
Defining application routes	17
Summary	20
Chapter 2: Configuring Routes - Using Various Options in the Route Component	23
Route props	24
The exact prop	24
The strict prop	25
The sensitive prop	26
Inline rendering with the render prop	27
Inline rendering with the children prop	28
Route component props	29
History	29
The location object	30
The match object	31
Route parameters	32
Nested routes and dynamic routing	34
Dynamic routes from JSON	37
Summary	39
Chapter 3: Using the Link and NavLink Components to Navigate to a Route	41
<Link> component	42
replace prop	43
innerRef prop	43
to prop with an object	44
<NavLink> component	46
activeClassName prop	46
activeStyle prop	46
exact prop	47
strict prop	48

Table of Contents

isActive prop	48
location prop	49
Navigating to nested routes	50
Navigating to a route programmatically using history	50
Using the withRouter higher-order component	51
Preventing transitions with <Prompt>	53
Summary	55
Chapter 4: Using the Redirect and Switch Components	57
The <Redirect> component	58
The to prop	58
The push prop	60
Protecting routes and authorization	61
Redirecting with a callback route	63
Exclusive routing with the <Switch> component	65
Ordering of the <Route> components in <Switch>	66
<Route> with path '/' as the first child in <Switch>	66
<Route> with path params	67
Adding a 404 – Page Not Found	67
Using <Redirect> in <Switch> to redirect to a Page Not Found page	69
Redirecting from an old path to a new path	70
Summary	71
Chapter 5: Understanding the Core Router, and Configuring the BrowserRouter and HashRouter components	73
<Router> component	74
Including <Router> from react-router	75
react-router package	76
react-router-dom package	77
<BrowserRouter> component	78
basename prop	79
forceRefresh prop	80
keyLengthprop	80
getUserConfirmation prop	81
Showing a custom dialog box using the getUserConfirmation prop	82
<HashRouter> component	86
hashType prop	87
Summary	88
Chapter 6: Using StaticRouter in a Server-Side Rendered React Application	89
Performing SSR of a React application using Node.js and Express.js	90
Installing dependencies	90
Webpack build configuration	91
Server-Side application	92
Rendering a React application using ReactDOMServer.renderToString	93

[ii]

Adding <StaticRouter> and creating routes	94
Server-Side redirect using the <Redirect> and staticContext	96
Request URL matching with matchPath	98
StaticRouter context prop	100
Creating Isomorphic React applications	102
Webpack configuration	104
Server-Side configuration	105
Summary	106
Chapter 7: Using NativeRouter in a React Native Application	107
Using NativeRouter in a React Native application	108
Creating a new project with the create-react-native-app CLI	108
Adding the <NativeRouter> component	110
The <NativeRouter> component	115
The initialEntries prop	116
The initialIndex prop	116
The <BackButton> component	117
Creating Deeplinks with <DeepLinking>	118
Ejecting from the create-react-native-app	119
Adding <intent-filter> to the manifest file	120
Including the <DeepLinking> component	122
Summary	123
Chapter 8: Redux Bindings with connected-react-router	125
State management with Redux	126
Actions	126
Reducers	127
Store	127
Redux in React	128
Getting started with connected-react-router	131
Reading state information from the Redux store	134
Navigating by dispatching actions	136
Summary	137
Other Books You May Enjoy	139
Index	143

[iii]

Preface

The React framework from Facebook redefines the way frontend applications should be built. React Router has become the de-facto routing framework for applications built with React. With its latest version 4 release, the library has been rewritten in React and it lets you handle routing declaratively. In this book, you'll learn how the react-router library can be used in any React application, including web and native mobile applications developed with React Native. The book also covers topics such as server-side routing and Redux integration with React Router.

Who this book is for

This book is for web and native mobile application developers who are considering building applications using React and React Router. A little knowledge of the React framework and JavaScript would be helpful in understanding the concepts discussed in this book.

What this book covers

Chapter 1, *Introduction to React Router 4 and Creating Your First Route*, is an introduction to the component-based architecture in React and how you can get started with creating routes using the `Route` component from React Router.

Chapter 2, *Configuring Routes – Using Various Options in the Route Component*, discusses various `Route` component props that can be used to match the requested URL location and how these matches can be used to render a component. Also, the chapter explains how routes can be added dynamically as the user traverses through the application.

Chapter 3, *Using the Link and NavLink Components to Navigate to a Route*, talks about how to use the `Link` and `NavLink` components in React Router to allow you to navigate to routes defined in the application. This chapter also explains about the higher-order component `withRouter` and how to prevent accidental transition using the `Prompt` component.

Chapter 4, *Using the Redirect and Switch Components*, goes into how to use the `Redirect` component to redirect the user to a different route and the `Switch` component to match one route and redirect the user to a `404 page not found` page if the requested location is not found.

Chapter 5, *Understanding the Core Router, and Configuring the BrowserRouter and HashRouter components*, is an in-depth explanation of how the core router interface is used to update the sections of the screen and the browser's history. The chapter also explains two router interfaces used in a web application: `BrowserRouter` and `HashRouter`.

Chapter 6, *Using StaticRouter in a Server-Side Rendered React Application*, explores how to use the `StaticRouter` component to provide routing features on a server-side-rendered application. The chapter also explains how `StaticRouter` and `BrowserRouter` can be used to build an isomorphic web application.

Chapter 7, *Using NativeRouter in a React Native Application*, details how to provide routing in a native mobile application developed with React Native using the `NativeRouter` component. The chapter also explains how you can integrate with the device's back button using the `BackButton` component and provide deep linking support using the `DeepLinking` component.

Chapter 8, *Redux Bindings with connected-react-router*, examines how to use the `connected-react-router` library, which provides Redux bindings for React Router; the chapter explains how to read routing information from the router state in the Redux store and how to navigate by dispatching actions to the store.

To get the most out of this book

React Router is used in web and native applications developed with React. The book assumes that you have a good understanding of JavaScript and some of the new language features introduced in ECMAScript 6, such as classes and spread operators.

The book provides a brief introduction to React and component-based architecture in React. Some of the other core concepts of React are documented at `https://reactjs.org`.

The book assumes that the reader has used Node.js and NPM to install libraries and packages from the NPM repository.

Download the example code files

You can download the example code files for this book from your account at `www.packt.com`. If you purchased this book elsewhere, you can visit `www.packt.com/support` and register to have the files emailed directly to you.

You can download the code files by following these steps:

1. Log in or register at www.packt.com
2. Select the **SUPPORT** tab
3. Click on **Code Downloads & Errata**
4. Enter the name of the book in the **Search** box and follow the onscreen instructions

Once the file is downloaded, please make sure that you unzip or extract the folder using the latest version of:

- WinRAR/7-Zip for Windows
- Zipeg/iZip/UnRarX for Mac
- 7-Zip/PeaZip for Linux

The code bundle for the book is also hosted on GitHub at https://github.com/PacktPublishing/React-Router-Quick-Start-Guide. In case there's an update to the code, it will be updated on the existing GitHub repository.

We also have other code bundles from our rich catalog of books and videos available at https://github.com/PacktPublishing/. Check them out!

Download the color images

We also provide a PDF file that has color images of the screenshots/diagrams used in this book. You can download it here: https://www.packtpub.com/sites/default/files/downloads/9781789532555_ColorImages.pdf.

Conventions used

There are a number of text conventions used throughout this book.

CodeInText: Indicates code words in text, database table names, folder names, filenames, file extensions, pathnames, dummy URLs, user input, and Twitter handles. Here is an example: "Mount the downloaded WebStorm-10*.dmg disk image file as another disk in your system."

Preface

A block of code is set as follows:

```
In GitHubComponent
GitHub ID - mjackson
```

When we wish to draw your attention to a particular part of a code block, the relevant lines or items are set in bold:

```
<Route
    to='/github/:githubID'
    component={GitHubComponent}
/>
```

Any command-line input or output is written as follows:

```
Root:
path: /category, isExact: true
```

Bold: Indicates a new term, an important word, or words that you see onscreen. For example, words in menus or dialog boxes appear in the text like this. Here is an example: "Select **System info** from the **Administration** panel."

Warnings or important notes appear like this.

Tips and tricks appear like this.

Get in touch

Feedback from our readers is always welcome.

General feedback: Email `feedback@packt.com` and mention the book title in the subject of your message. If you have questions about any aspect of this book, please email us at `questions@packt.com`.

Errata: Although we have taken every care to ensure the accuracy of our content, mistakes do happen. If you have found a mistake in this book, we would be grateful if you would report this to us. Please visit www.packt.com/submit-errata, selecting your book, clicking on the Errata Submission Form link, and entering the details.

Piracy: If you come across any illegal copies of our works in any form on the Internet, we would be grateful if you would provide us with the location address or website name. Please contact us at copyright@packt.com with a link to the material.

If you are interested in becoming an author: If there is a topic that you have expertise in and you are interested in either writing or contributing to a book, please visit authors.packtpub.com.

Reviews

Please leave a review. Once you have read and used this book, why not leave a review on the site that you purchased it from? Potential readers can then see and use your unbiased opinion to make purchase decisions, we at Packt can understand what you think about our products, and our authors can see your feedback on their book. Thank you!

For more information about Packt, please visit packtpub.com.

Introduction to React Router 4 and Creating Your First Route

Single page applications (**SPAs**) have become the de facto standard for developing applications for the web. Many JavaScript libraries and frameworks have emerged that help frontend engineers in developing SPAs. These include React, Angular, Ember, and Backbone, to name a few. These libraries or frameworks abstract native APIs and provide services and components that can be used to build applications quicker. SPAs are an excellent choice for providing a fluid user experience; as the user traverses through the site, HTTP requests are triggered, and only certain sections of the page are updated, instead of requesting the server for the entire page.

React is an open source JavaScript library that helps you in building user interfaces and the view layer in web and mobile applications. It encourages developers to visualize the view layer as a collection of components that can be reused throughout the application. Most frontend frameworks include a routing package that enables you to update sections of the page when the user clicks through various links provided on the site. A router in a frontend framework listens to the changes in the URL and keeps the application in sync by rendering the corresponding view components. For example, when the user visits `'/dashboard'`, the page would render various dashboard components, such as charts and tables, and when the user visits, say, `'/user'`, the page would list various user attributes. In a React-based application, a Router library is required, since React does not ship with one. React-Router is one such popular routing library built completely with React. The library includes various components that can be used to render views as the user navigates through the application. Apart from matching the URL and rendering the view components, React-Router has several features that help you to configure the routes easily.

In this chapter, the following topics are discussed:

- A brief look at React: This section introduces you to some of the core concepts in React, such as component-based architecture, creating components in React, and how data can be provided to child components in the application tree
- Introduction to React-Router: Here, we first create a React application using the `create-react-app` CLI and then add the React-Router library (the `'react-router-dom'` package) as a dependency
- Creating your first route: After adding React-Router as a dependency, the application's first route is created using the `<BrowserRouter>` and `<Route>` components

A brief look at React

React is a JavaScript library that provides a set of components and services and enables you to build user interfaces.

Here is a quote from `reactjs.org`:

> "React is a declarative, efficient, and flexible JavaScript library for building user interfaces."

The library is developed and maintained by Facebook and is licensed under MIT. It's extensively used in building various applications at Facebook, including Facebook web and Instagram web.

React enables you to build view components that get updated when the application's state changes. The state here could refer to the underlying domain data, or it may reflect where the user is in the application journey. React ensures that the view components reflect the application state.

Here are some of the important features of React:

- **JSX**: Components in React applications use an XML/HTML-like syntax, known as JSX, to render the view elements. JSX allows you to include HTML in your JavaScript/React code; the familiar syntax of HTML with attributes in your React component's render function does not require you to learn a new templating language. This JSX is then used by preprocessors such as Babel to transpile HTML text to JavaScript objects that the JavaScript engine can understand.

- **One-way data binding**: React applications are organized as a series of nested components; a set of immutable values are passed to the component's renderer as properties in HTML tags. The component does not modify the properties (or props) it receives from its parent; instead, the child communicates the user actions to its parent component and the parent component modifies these properties by updating the component's state.
- **Virtual DOM**: In React, for every DOM object, a corresponding virtual DOM object is created that has the same set of properties as the real DOM object. However, the virtual DOM object lacks the power to update the view when the user interacts with the page. Components in React re-render the view elements whenever a change in state is detected, and this re-render updates the virtual DOM tree. React then compares this virtual DOM tree with the snapshot that was created before the update to determine the DOM objects that changed. Finally, React modifies the real DOM by updating only those DOM objects that changed.

Component-based architecture in React

Since its release in 2013, React has redefined the way that frontend applications should be built. It introduces the concept of component-based architecture, which, in essence, allows you to visualize your application as if it were made up of tiny, self-sustained view components. These view components are reusable; that is, a component such as `CommentBox` or `Footer` encapsulates the necessary functionality and can be used across the pages in the site.

A page in this context is itself a view component that is composed of other tiny view components, as shown here:

```
<Dashboard>
    <Header>
        <Brand />
    </Header>
    <SideNav>
        <NavLink key="1">
        <NavLink key="2">
    </SideNav>
    <ContentArea>
        <Chart>
        <Grid data="stockPriceList">
    </ContentArea>
    <Footer />
</Dashboard>
```

Here, `<Dashboard>` is a view component that encompasses several other view components (`Header`, `SideNav`, `ContentArea`, and `Footer`), which in turn are made up tiny components (`Brand`, `NavLink`, `Chart`, and `Grid`). The component-based architecture encourages you to build components that provide certain functionality and are not tightly coupled with any of their parent or sibling components. These components implement certain functionality and provide an interface through which they can be included in the page.

In the preceding example, a `<Grid>` component would include features such as rendering data in rows and columns, providing search functionality, and also an option to sort the columns either in ascending or descending order. The `<Grid>` component would implement all of the aforementioned features and provide an interface through which it can be included in the page. The interface here would include the tag name (`Grid`) and set of properties (`props`) that accept the values from its parent component. Here, the `<Grid>` component could interface with the backend system and retrieve the data; however, this would make the component tied tightly to the given backend interface, thus not making it reusable. Ideally, a view component would receive data from its parent component and act accordingly:

```
<Grid data="stockPriceList" />
```

Here, the `<Grid>` component receives a list containing stock price information through its `data` prop and would render this information in a tabular format. A component that includes this `<Grid>` component can be termed a `Container` component and `Grid` as a child component.

A `Container` component is also a `View` component; however, its responsibility includes providing its child components with the necessary data to render. A `Container` component could initiate HTTP calls to a backend service and receive the data required to render its child components. In addition to that, the `Container` component is also responsible for the positioning of the individual view components in its view area.

Creating a React component

A React component is created by extending the `Component` class provided by React as follows:

```
import React, { Component } from 'react';
import './button.css';

export class Button extends Component {
    render() {
```

```
        return (
            <button className={this.props.type}>
                {this.props.children}
            </button>
        );
    }
}
```

Here, the `Button` class extends React's `Component` class and overrides the `render` method. The `render` method returns the JSX, which will be rendered on the DOM when the page loads. The `type` and `children` properties are available in `this.props`. React allows you to pass data to its components through props and does so by using the following syntax:

```
import React, { Component } from 'react';
import { Button } from './components/Button/button';
import './App.css';

export default class App extends Component {
    render() {
        return (
            <div className="App">
                <Button type="secondary">CANCEL</Button>
                <Button type="primary">OK</Button>
            </div>
        );
    }
}
```

Here, we have wrapped the `Button` component inside a parent component, `App`, to render two button elements. The `type` attribute is consumed by the `Button` component to set the class name (`className`) of the `CANCEL` and `OK` buttons and text mentioned inside the `Button` tag. This can be referenced using the `children` property. The `children` property can be plain text or other view components. The child component gets a reference to the data provided by its parent component using `this.props`. The `children` property in `'this.props'` provides a reference to all the child elements included between the tags by the parent component. If you've used Angular in the past, consider the preceding snippet as similar to how you would include elements using `ng-transclude` in AngularJS, or `ng-content` in Angular.

Here, the `<App>` component contains the `<Button>` component and can be referred to as a container component, which is responsible for rendering the buttons on the page.

The next step is to render the `<App>` component on the DOM. The `<App>` component serves as a root component, that is, a root node in a tree. Every component in the application has the `<App>` component as its top-most parent component:

```
import React from 'react';
import ReactDOM from 'react-dom';
import App from './App';
import './index.css';

ReactDOM.render(<App />, document.getElementById('root'));
```

This code is included in `index.js`, which imports the `React` and `ReactDOM` libraries. The `ReactDOM` library has a `render` method, which accepts the component to be rendered as its first parameter, and a reference to the DOM node where the root component has to be rendered.

When the app is run, the content inside the `<App>` component is rendered:

```
▼<div id="root">
  ▼<div class="App">
     <button class="secondary">CANCEL</button>
     <button class="primary">OK</button>
   </div>
 </div>
```

Introduction to React-Router

React-Router is a routing library for SPAs built with React. React-Router version 4 is a complete rewrite and embraces the React philosophy of component-based architecture.

This is from the React-Router documentation (https://reacttraining.com/react-router/)

> "React Router is a collection of **navigational components** that compose declaratively with your application. Whether you want to have **bookmarkable URLs** for your web app or a composable way to navigate in **React Native**, React Router works wherever React is rendering--so take your pick!"

React-Router can be used wherever React can be applied; that is, React-Router works both in the browser and in the native environment with React Native.

The library is divided into three packages:

- `react-router`: Common core components for DOM and Native versions
- `react-router-dom`: Components for use in browser and web applications
- `react-router-native`: Components for use in native applications built with React Native

The library provides various components that can be used to add routes dynamically to your application. The dynamic routing in React-Router v4 allows you to specify application routes as the user progresses through the application journey. Frameworks such as AngularJS and Express require you to specify the routes upfront, and this routing information is required when the application bootstraps. In fact, the earlier versions of React-Router followed the same paradigm and required the routing configuration to be available upfront.

Apart from dynamic routing and providing fluid navigation in a React application, the library includes various features that are available in traditional websites. These include the following:

- Navigating backward and forward through the application, maintaining the history, and restoring the state of the application
- Rendering appropriate page components when presented with a URL (deep-linking)
- Redirecting the user from one route to the other
- Support for rendering a 404 page when none of the routes match the URL
- Support for hash-based routes and pretty URLs with HTML5 mode

It's a common misconception that React-Router is the official routing solution provided by Facebook. In reality, it's a third-party library and is licensed under MIT.

Getting started with React-Router

Let's create a React application and then add React-Router as a dependency.

To create a React application, we will use the `create-react-app` CLI. The `create-react-app` CLI makes it easier to create an application that already works. The CLI creates a project scaffold so that you can start using the latest JavaScript features, and also provides scripts to build applications for a production environment. There are various React and React-Router starter kits available; however, using `create-react-app` helps in demonstrating how React-Router can be added to an existing bare-bones React application.

The first step is to install `create-react-app` globally using NPM, as follows:

```
npm install -g create-react-app
```

The CLI requires the `node` version to be greater than or equal to 6, and the `npm` version to be greater than 5.2.0.

Once the CLI has been installed, we will create a new application using the `create-react-app` command, as seen here:

```
create-react-app react-router-demo-app
```

The following output is displayed when `create-react-app` completes the installation of packages:

```
Inside that directory, you can run several commands:
   npm start
      Starts the development server.

   npm run build
      Bundles the app into static files for production.

   npm test
      Starts the test runner.

   npm run eject
      Removes this tool and copies build dependencies, configuration
      files
      and scripts into the app directory. If you do this, you can't
       go back!
    We suggest that you begin by typing:
    cd react-router-demo-app
    npm start
```

If you used the `yarn` package manager (https://yarnpkg.com/en/), the `npm` commands in the preceding snippet would be replaced with `yarn`.

The `react-router-demo-app` directory is created during installation (if it doesn't already exist). Inside the directory, the following project structure is created:

```
/react-router-demo-app
    |--node_modules
    |--public
    |    |--favicon.ico
    |    |--index.html
    |    |--manifest.json
    |--src
    |    |--App.css
    |    |--App.js
    |    |--App.test.js
    |    |--index.css
    |    |--index.js
    |    |--logo.svg
    |    |--registerServiceWorker.js
    |--package-lock.json
    |--package.json
    |--README.md
```

The CLI installs all the necessary dependencies, such as Babel, to transpile ES6 code to ES5, thus enabling you to leverage the latest JavaScript features. It also creates a build pipeline configuration with the help of webpack. Post-installation, no additional configuration is required to start or build the app. As noted in the preceding output, you can start the app using the `npm start` command and build a production-ready app using `npm build`.

Introduction to React Router 4 and Creating Your First Route

On running `npm start`, the application is compiled and will open a browser window with a **Welcome to React** message displayed, as shown here:

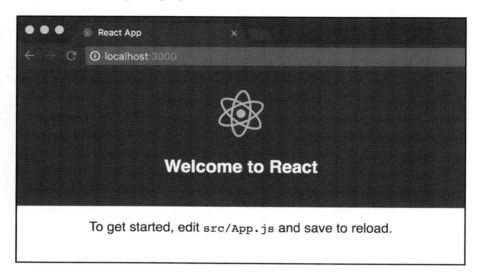

In the `index.js` file, the `ReactDOM` reference is used to render the application's root component as follows:

```
ReactDOM.render(<App />, document.getElementById('root'));
```

The `<App>` component marks the beginning of the tree that will get rendered when the application starts.

Adding the React-Router library

Now that we have our sample application up and running, let's add React-Router library as a dependency using `npm`:

```
npm install --save react-router-dom
```

This command will download and add `react-router-dom` to the `/node_modules` directory. The `package.json` file now includes this as a dependency:

```
"dependencies": {
  "react": "^16.4.0",
  "react-dom": "^16.4.0",
  "react-router-dom": "^4.3.0",
  "react-scripts": "1.1.4"
}
```

At the time of writing this book, version 4.3.0 of `react-router-dom` was available. You can try the alpha and beta builds by mentioning `react-router-dom@next` when including the library using `npm`.

Defining application routes

The `react-router-dom` package includes a `<BrowserRouter>` component, which is used as a wrapper before adding routes in the application. To use React-Router in the React Native application, the `react-router-native` package is used. This will be discussed in detail in later chapters. The `<BrowserRouter>` component is an implementation of the router interface that makes use of HTML5's history API to keep the UI in sync with the URL path.

The first step is to wrap the application's root component with `<BrowserRouter>`, as shown here:

```
import { BrowserRouter } from 'react-router-dom';

ReactDOM.render(
    <BrowserRouter>
        <App />
    </BrowserRouter>,
    document.getElementById('root')
);
```

Wrapping your application inside `<BrowserRouter>` will create an instance of history for our `<App>` component, giving all of its child components access to props from the native browser history API. This allows components to match against URL paths and render the appropriate page component.

[17]

Introduction to React Router 4 and Creating Your First Route

 History is a JavaScript library that lets you manage history stack navigation and helps in persisting state between sessions.

Routing in React-Router isn't actually routing—it's conditional rendering of components based on the pattern that matches with the current URL path. To define a route, we need two pieces of information: the URL path to match with and the component to render. Let's create two components, `HomeComponent` and `DashboardComponent`, that render at `/home` and `/dashboard` respectively.

In `src/components/home/home.component.js`:

```
import React from 'react';

export const HomeComponent = () => (
    <div>
        Inside Home route
    </div>
);
```

And in `src/components/dashboard/dashboard.component.js`:

```
import React from 'react';

export const DashboardComponent = () => (
    <div className="dashboard">
        Inside Dashboard route
    </div>
);
```

The `import` statement is required since we are returning JSX from the preceding components.

The next step is to define a route using the `Route` component (from `'react-router-dom'`). The `Route` component accepts several props, but for the purpose of this example, we will use `path` and `component`.

In `App.js`:

```
class App extends Component {
    render() {
        return (
            <div className="container">
                <Route
                    path="/home"
                    component={HomeComponent}
                />
                <Route
                    path="/dashboard"
                    component={DashboardComponent}
                />
            </div>
        );
    }
}

export default App;
```

Here, we're defining routes within the `'render'` method of the `<App>` component. Each `<Route>` component has a `path` prop, which mentions the URL path to match, and a `component` prop, mentioning the component to render once the path matches the URL.

In the preceding example, the component was created without extending React's component class. If a component, created by extending React's component class, is provided as a value to the `component` prop, then the component's lifecycle methods, `componentWillMount` and `componentWillUnmount`, are called every time that `<Route>` renders the component.

When you run the app (`npm start`) and visit `localhost:3000/home`, `HomeComponent` is rendered and the message **Inside Home Component** is displayed.
Similarly, `DashboardComponent` is rendered when you visit `localhost:3000/dashboard`.

`<BrowserRouter>` creates a `History` object, which it uses to keep track of the current location and re-render the site whenever it changes. `<BrowserRouter>` makes the `History` object available to its descendent child components through React's context. A `Route` component that does not have `<BrowserRouter>` as its parent will fail to work.

Also, it's a requirement that `<BrowserRouter>` has only one child element. In the following snippet, `<BrowserRouter>` is given two child elements:

```
<BrowserRouter>
    <Route
        path="/home"
        component={HomeComponent} />
    <Route
        path="/dashboard"
        component={DashboardComponent} />
</BrowserRouter>
```

The preceding code will result in an error, such as **A <Router> may have only one child element**. To resolve this, you could either move these routes into a component and provide the component reference, or wrap the `<Route>` components in the preceding snippet inside another element, such as `div` or `React Fragment`.

A `React fragment` is used to group a list of children without adding extra nodes to the DOM. A fragment is used when the component returns multiple elements.

Apart from `BrowserRouter`, there are other types of routers in the React-Router library: `HashRouter`, `MemoryRouter`, and `StaticRouter`. These are discussed in later chapters.

Summary

React is a JavaScript library used to build user interfaces. Unlike libraries such as Angular and Ember, which include a routing package, the React library does not include any components or services that help in routing. React-Router is a routing library that can be used in any React application, web or native. React-Router version 4 is a complete rewrite of the earlier versions and all of its components are written in React. The library includes the packages `react-router-dom` for use in web applications; `react-router-native`, for use in native applications built with React-Native; and `react-router`, a core package that both `react-router-dom` and `react-router-native` have a dependency on.

The `create-react-app` CLI is used to quickly scaffold a React application. It includes build configuration scripts that can be used to generate builds for development and production environments. The `react-router-dom` package is then added as a dependency to the application. The package includes the `<BrowserRouter>` component, which implements a `History` interface. The application's root component, `<App />`, is wrapped inside React-Router's `<BrowserRouter>` component to make the `History` object available to all the components in the application tree.

To create our first route, the `<Route>` component is included. It accepts `path` and `component` as props, and renders the component when the browser's URL matches the `<Route>` path.

In `Chapter 2`, *Configuring Routes - Using Various Options in the Route Component*, the `<Route>` component props are discussed in detail. Also, we will take a look at the various props that the rendered component receives, and consider how these props can be used to create nested routes.

2
Configuring Routes - Using Various Options in the Route Component

React-Router allows you to declaratively define routes using the `<Route>` component. It's the main building block of React-Router, and renders the component mentioned in the `component` prop when the path value mentioned in the `path` prop matches the browser's URL location. The `<Route>` component, like any other React component, accepts a set of props. These props provide more granular control over how the browser's URL path should match the `<Route>` component's path, and a couple of other rendering options as well.

In the previous chapter, we briefly saw how a `<Route>` component is used to match the URL path and render a component. In this chapter, we will take a look at the following:

- A deep dive into various props that can be added to a `<Route>` component, such as `exact`, `strict`, `render`, `children`, and `sensitive`.
- **Route component props**: the component, which gets rendered as a result of a `<Route>` path match, receives data as props that can then be used to create nested routes.
- **Route parameters**: The `<Route>` component's path can be configured to accept additional params from the URL segment, and these params can be read in the rendered component.
- **Nested or dynamic routes**: a `<Route>` component can be added inside a rendered component instead of defining routes at the application level. The rendered component thus provides the next step in the application journey.
- **Generating routes from JSON configuration**: Route information available in the JSON object can be used to add routes to the application.

Route props

When you look at the source code of React-Router, the `<Route>` component accepts the following props:

```
Route.propTypes = {
    computedMatch: PropTypes.object, // private, from <Switch>
    path: PropTypes.string,
    exact: PropTypes.bool,
    strict: PropTypes.bool,
    sensitive: PropTypes.bool,
    component: PropTypes.func,
    render: PropTypes.func,
    children: PropTypes.oneOfType([PropTypes.func, PropTypes.node]),
    location: PropTypes.object
};
```

Let's take a look at each of these props in the following section.

The exact prop

In our previous `<Route>` example, let's change the `'/home'` route path to `'/'`, as shown here:

```
<div className="container">
    <Route
        path="/"
        component={HomeComponent}
    />
    <Route
        path="/dashboard"
        component={DashboardComponent}
    />
</div>
```

With these routes in place, when the browser's URL is set to /dashboard, you'll notice that the content from both components is displayed as follows:

> Inside Home route
> Inside Dashboard route

Here, the '/' in '/dashboard' matches both of the <Route> paths, '/' and '/dashboard'; therefore it renders content from both the components. To match the browser's location.pathname exactly with the <Route> component's path, add the exact prop to the <Route>, as shown here:

```
..
  <Route
      path="/"
      component={HomeComponent}
      exact
  />
..
```

Similarly, when you try to access the '/dashboard' and '/dashboard/portfolio' paths, you'll notice that in both instances, DashboardComponent is rendered. To prevent '/dashboard/portfolio' from matching the <Route> component with the '/dashboard' path, add the exact prop.

> React-Router uses the path-to-regexp library internally to determine whether a route element's path prop matches the current location.

The strict prop

When the <Route> path has a trailing slash, and you would like to match this path, including the trailing slash, with the browser's URL, then include the strict prop. For example, after changing the <Route> path from '/dashboard' to '/dashboard/', the <Route> component would still match the URL path without the trailing slash. In other words, '/dashboard' would match the <Route> component with the '/dashboard/' path.

However, after adding the `strict` prop, React-Router ensures that `<Route>` matches only if the URL has a trailing slash:

```
<Route
    path="/dashboard/"
    component={DashboardComponent}
    strict
/>
```

With this `<Route>` configuration in place, the `'/dashboard'` path would not match. However, when you add a trailing slash to the URL, as in `'/dashboard/'`, the `<Route>` component with a `strict` prop will match and the `DashboardComponent` would be rendered.

Please note, if you mention additional URL segments, then it would still match the `path` prop mentioned in the `<Route>` component. For example, if the URL path is `'/dashboard/123'`, it would match the `'/dashboard/'` path with a `<Route>` component that has the `strict` prop. To match a path including the additional URL segments, you can specify the `exact` prop along with the `strict` prop.

The sensitive prop

A `<Route>` component's path is not case-sensitive, that is, a `<Route>` component with its path prop value set to `'/Dashboard'` would match the `'/dashboard'` or `'/DASHBOARD'` URL path. To make a `<Route>` component's path case-sensitive, add the `sensitive` prop:

```
<Route
    path="/Dashboard"
    component={DashboardComponent}
    sensitive
/>
```

The `sensitive` prop ensures that the path prop's case is taken into consideration when matching it with the browser's URL path. By adding the `sensitive` prop, one can define routes with the same pathname, but do so using a different case:

```
<Route
    path="/Dashboard"
    component={DashboardComponent}
    sensitive
/>
<Route
    path="/dashboard"
    component={StockListComponent}
    sensitive
/>
```

This code would create two distinct routes and would render the corresponding component when the `<Route>` component's case-sensitive path matches the browser's URL path.

Inline rendering with the render prop

We have already taken a look at how the `component` prop can be used to render a view when the `<Route>` path matches the browser's `location.pathname`. There are two other props available to render a view: `render` and `children`.

The `render` prop is used for inline rendering. The function mentioned as a value to the `render` prop should return a React element similar to the following:

```
<Route
    path="/user"
    render={() => (
        <div> Inside User Route </div>
    )}
/>
```

From the preceding code snippet, when the `'/user'` path matches the browser's URL, the function specified as a value to the `render` prop is executed, and the React element returned from this function is rendered.

> When you specify both `component` and `render` props in the same `<Route>` component, the `component` prop will take precedence.

[27]

Inline rendering with the children prop

The `children` prop should be used in a case where you want to render the view irrespective of whether or not there's a path match. The syntax for the `children` prop is similar to the `render` prop, as shown here:

```
<Route
    path="/sidenav"
    children={() => (
        <div> Inside Sidenav route </div>
    )}
/>
```

The `<Route>` component with a `children` prop is rendered even if the `path` prop is not specified. Also, the `exact` and `strict` props will not have any effect on a `<Route>` component with a `children` prop.

Both the `component` and `render` props take precedence over the `children` prop. Also, when either the `component` or `render` props are mentioned, the view is rendered only if the path matches the requested URL.

A `<Route>` component with a `children` prop is rendered based on its position in the list of routes. For example, if the previous `<Route>` component is specified as the last entry in the list of routes, then it is rendered after all the preceding matching routes have been rendered. Also, if the previous `<Route>` component is listed before the matching route, then the route's content is rendered before rendering the matching route's content, as seen here:

```
<Route
    path="/sidenav"
    children={() => (
        <div> Inside Sidenav route </div>
    )}
/>

<Route
    path="/user"
    render={() => (
        <div> Inside User route </div>
    )}
/>
```

Here, when you try to access the `'/user'` path, the `<Route>` component with a `children` prop is rendered before rendering the route with the `'/user'` path.

Route component props

The component that gets rendered when the `<Route>` path matches the browser's URL path receives certain `props`, such as `history`, `location`, `match`, and `staticContext`. The data provided by these props includes information pertaining to the route. The props are available to the component that gets rendered using the `component`, `render`, or `children` props of the `<Route>` component.

The `staticContext` property is set when you are rendering the application on the server side and it is not available (as in, set to `undefined`) in the client-side router that is, when using the `<BrowserRouter>` interface. Server-side rendering of the application is covered in the upcoming chapters.

History

React-Router has a dependency on the `history` package. `history` is a JavaScript library used in maintaining sessions in any JavaScript application. Consider the following quote from history's documentation (`https://github.com/ReactTraining/history`):

> "**history** *is a JavaScript library that lets you easily manage session history anywhere JavaScript runs. history abstracts away the differences in various environments and provides a minimal API that lets you manage the history stack, navigate, confirm navigation, and persist state between sessions.*"

The `history` object has several properties and methods:

- **action**: The current action, `PUSH`, `POP`, or `REPLACE`
- **length**: The count of entries in the history stack
- **location**: The current location, which includes the `hash`, `pathname`, `search`, and `state` properties
    - **hash**: Hash fragment
    - **pathname**: URL path
    - **search**: URL query string
    - **state**: The state information provided when navigating from one route to the other using `location.pushState`
- `block()`: A function that registers a prompt message that will be displayed when the user tries to navigate away from the current page.

- `createHref()`: A function that constructs a URL segment; it accepts an object with the `pathname`, `search`, and `hash` properties.
- `go(n)`: A function that navigates through the history stack. `history.go(-1)` moves the pointer back by one position and `history.go(1)` moves the pointer forward by one position in the `history` stack.
- `goBack()`: A function that navigates the pointer back by one position in the `history` stack; the same as `history.go(-1)`.
- `goForward()`: A function that navigates the pointer forward by one position in the `history` stack; the same as `history.go(1)`.
- `listen(listenerFn)`: A function that registers a listener function that gets called whenever there's a change in `history.location`.
- `push(path, state?)`: A function that navigates to the given pathname, adding an entry to the `history` stack. It optionally accepts a `state` parameter, which can be used to pass application state data.
- `replace(path, state?)`: A function that navigates to the given pathname, replacing the current entry in the `history` stack. It also accepts an optional `state` parameter.

The `history` object is used by React-Router internally to update the entries in the history stack when the user tries to navigate between pages. It's provided to the rendered component as a prop so that the user can be navigated to different pages using the aforementioned methods in the `history` object. In the next chapter, we will take a look at various APIs provided by React-Router that help you navigate to different routes defined in the application.

The location object

The `location` object gives a snapshot of data representing the current state of the application. It includes the following properties: `pathname`, `hash`, `search`, and `state`. The navigation components can provide values to these props, which can then be read by the rendered component that matches the browser's URL. As mentioned previously, we will take a look at various navigation components in Chapter3, *Using Link and NavLink Components to Navigate to a Route*.

The location information is also found in the `history` object; however, the `history` object is mutable, and thus, accessing the location in the `history` object should be avoided.

The match object

The `match` object contains information on how the `<Route>` path matches the current URL. It includes the `url`, `path`, `isExact`, and `params` properties.

Let's refer to one of the earlier routes where the `render` prop is used:

```
<Route
    path="/user"
    render={({ match }) => {
        console.log(match);
        return (
            <div> Inside User route </div>
        );
    }}
/>
```

When you try accessing the `/user` path, the `match` object's properties will have the following values:

```
url - '/user'
path - '/user'
params - {}
isExact - true
```

- `url`: A string that returns the matched portion of the URL
- `path`: A string that returns the route's path string, that is, the path pattern mentioned in the `<Route>` component's path prop
- `params`: An object containing a list of path params passed to the route (there will be more on params in the upcoming sections)
- `isExact`: A Boolean value; this is `true` if the URL matches the provided `path` prop in its entirety

The `isExact` property is `false` if only a part of the URL segment matches the `<Route>` component's path. For example, the `<Route>` component with the `/user` path doesn't match the URL of `/user/123` in its entirety, and in this case, `isExact` is false.

As mentioned earlier, a `<Route>` component with a `children` prop is rendered irrespective of whether or not the `path` prop matches the browser's URL path. Here, the `match` object would be set to null if the path does not match the URL segment:

```
<Route
    path="/sidenav"
    children={({ match }) => {
        console.log(match)
```

[31]

```
        return (
            <div> Inside Sidenav route </div>
        );
    }}
/>
```

With this `<Route>` configuration, when you try to access the `/user` path, the `<Route>` component with the `/sidenav` path is matched, since it has a `children` prop. However, here the `match` object is set to null. This helps in determining whether a path matched the URL segment or not for a `<Route>` component with a `children` prop.

Route parameters

A `<Route>` component in React-Router can be configured to accept URL parameters that change for a given object. For example, to display user information for a given `userID`, the URL path could look like `'/user/1'` for a user with a `userID` of `'1'`, and `'/user/123'` for a user with a `userID` of `'123'`. The last portion of the URL is dynamic; however, in each instance, the rendered component would perform the same operation for a given `userID`.

An example of such a use case is Twitter's profile page. The page accepts `twitterID` and displays the feed for the given user.

A `<Route>` component can be configured to accept the dynamic portion in the URL by appending an additional path in the `'to'` prop, prefixed with a colon (:) as seen here:

```
<Route
    to='/github/:githubID'
    component={GitHubComponent}
/>
```

Here, the `'/:githubID'` path is dynamic, and can match paths such as `'/github/ryanflorence'` and `'/github/mjackson'` (the GitHub IDs of the creators of React-Router).

These matched URL parameters can then be consumed in the rendered component using `match.params`:

```
export class GitHubComponent extends Component {
    render() {
        const { match: { params } } = this.props;
        return (
            <div>
```

```
            In GitHubComponent <br />
            GitHub ID - {params.githubID}
        </div>
    )
  }
}
```

When you try accessing the '/github/mjackson' URL path, you'll see this message:

```
In GitHubComponent
GitHub ID - mjackson
```

The match.params object contains key-value pairs of the matching params in the route. The <Route> component can also accept multiple params in the URL, as shown here:

```
<Route
    path="/github/:githubID/:twitterID"
    component={GitHubComponent}
/>
```

Here, the githubID and twitterID params are dynamic and can match URL paths such as '/github/ryanflorence/mjackson'. The second param, twitterID, can be read in the component using match.params.twitterID.

In the previous <Route> configuration, the githubID and twitterID params are required params, that is, the route won't match if both the params are not present in the URL path. To mark a param as optional, suffix the param with a question mark (?), as shown in the following snippet:

```
<Route
    path="/github/:githubID/:twitterID?"
    component={GitHubComponent}
/>
```

In the preceding <Route> configuration, the twitterID param is marked as optional. This means that when you try to access the '/github/ryanflorence' path, that is, access the path without providing a value to the twitterID param in the URL, then the path will match the URL and the component will be rendered. However, when the component tries to access the param using match.params.twitterID, it will return undefined.

The `<Route>` path can also be configured to accept params that match a regular expression, as shown here:

```
...
<Route
    path="/github/:githubID(\w+)"
    component={GitHubComponent}
/>
<Route
    path="/user/:userID(\d+)"
    component={UserComponent}
/>
...
```

Here, the `githubID` param is restricted to alphanumeric strings, and the `userID` param is restricted to numeric values. The param is suffixed with a regex pattern to define the kind of values that the `<Route>` param would accept, that is, a pattern that restricts the values that can be provided to the param.

Nested routes and dynamic routing

The earlier versions of React-Router required the routes to be defined upfront, and the child routes to be nested inside another route, as seen here:

```
<Router>
    <Route path='/' component={Container}>
        <IndexRoute component={Home} />
        <Route path='user' component={User}>
            <IndexRoute component={Twitter} />
            <Route path='instagram' component={Instagram} />
        </Route>
    </Route>
</Router>
```

This code can be considered static routing, wherein the route configuration is required by the library when the application initializes. Here, the route with the `'/'` path serves as the parent of all the routes, and the route with the `'user'` path is a child route of `'/'`, and a parent route for the route with the `'instagram'` path.

In React-Router v4, nested routes can be defined inside the rendered components, that is, routes get registered as the user navigates through the application. With the rewrite in v4, `<Route>` is a React component, and thus can be included in any component's `render` method.

Consider a parent route as defined in `App.js` (the `<App />` root component):

```
<Route
    path="/category"
    component={CategoryComponent}
/>
```

Here, the `'/category'` path is mapped to the `CategoryComponent` component.

`CategoryComponent` can, in turn, render other routes using the same `<Route>` component. However, when defining routes inside the rendered component (`CategoryComponent`), a reference to the current matching URL is required to be specified in the `<Route>` component's `to` prop. For example, a sub route with a `'/pictures'` path can be created using a `<Route>` component; however, an absolute path needs to be specified in the `to` prop, that is, `'/category/pictures'` or, more generally, `'/<current_matching_url>/pictures'`.

As mentioned earlier, the `match` prop passed to the rendered component contains information on how the path matched the current URL. The `match` prop's URL property can be used to refer to the parent URL:

```
export const CategoryComponent = ({ match }) => {
    return (
        <div className="nested-route-container">
            <div className="root-info">
                <h4> Root: </h4>
                <h5> path: {match.path}, isExact: {match.isExact.toString()}</h5>
            </div>
            <Route
                path={`${match.url}/pictures`}
                render={({ match }) => {
                    return (
                        <div>
                            <h4> Viewing pictures: </h4>
                            <h5>
                                path: {match.path},
                                isExact:
                                {match.isExact.toString()}
                            </h5>
                        </div>
                    )
                }}
            />
            <Route
                path={`${match.url}/books`}
```

Configuring Routes - Using Various Options in the Route Component

```
            render={({ match }) => {
                return (
                    <div>
                        <h4> Viewing books: </h4>
                        <h5>
                            path: {match.path},
                            isExact:
                            {match.isExact.toString()}
                        </h5>
                        <Route
                    path={`${match.url}/popular`}
                            render={({ match }) => (
                                <div>
                                    Inside popular,
                                    path:
                                    {match.path}
                                </div>
                            )} />
                    </div>
                )
            }}
        />
    </div>
    )
}
```

The `CategoryComponent` defined in the preceding snippet accepts the `match` prop, and the routes defined in the component have path values in the format of `'${match.url}/<child_route_path>'`. The `match.url` template variable contains the parent route's URL value, in this case, `/category`. Using the same principle, routes with the paths of `'/category/pictures'` and `'/category/books'` are also defined.

Let's test these routes:

- **Scenario 1**: `location.pathname` is `'/category'`:

    Here, the parent route is rendered and the page will render the route information as follows:

    ```
    Root:
    path: /category, isExact: true
    ```

    Here, `match.isExact` is true, since there are no additional URL segments after the `/category` path.

[36]

- **Scenario 2:** `location.pathname` is `'/category/pictures'` or `'/category/books'`:

  After rendering the `'/category'` parent route, the library looks for `<Route>` components with the paths of `'/category/pictures'` and `'/category/books'`. It finds one and renders the corresponding component:

  ```
  Root:
  path: /category, isExact: false
  Viewing pictures:
  path: /category/pictures, isExact: true
  ```

  Now, `match.isExact` in the parent route (a `<Route>` component with a `'/category'` path) is false; however, it's true in the child route.

- **Scenario 3**: `location.pathname` is `'/category/books/popular'`:

  It's possible to nest as many routes as you wish. Here, `'/books'` is a nested route, and also has another nested route, `'/popular'`, which matches the `'/category/books/popular'` path:

  ```
  Root:path: /category,
   isExact: false
   Viewing books:
  path: /category/books, isExact: false
  Inside popular,
  path: /category/books/popular
  ```

  The `match` prop is very useful in creating nested routes. These nested routes become accessible only when their parent route is rendered, allowing you to add your routes dynamically.

Dynamic routes from JSON

A set of `<Route>` components can also be generated by looking up an array containing a collection of route configuration options. Each route option should contain the necessary details, such as `'path'` and `'component'`.

Configuring Routes - Using Various Options in the Route Component

A collection of routes could look like the following:

```
const STOCK_ROUTES = [
    {
        path: 'stats',
        component: StatsComponent,
    },
    {
        path: 'news',
        component: NewsComponent
    },
    {
        path: 'trending',
        component: TrendingComponent
    }
];
```

Each object in the preceding array contains a `'path'` key specifying the route path, and a `'component'` key containing a reference to the component that you want to render when the user visits the route. The preceding collection can then be used inside the component's `render` method to generate a list of `<Route>` components, as follows:

```
...
render() {
    const { match } = this.props;
    return (
        <div>
            Inside Stocks, try /stocks/stats or /stocks/news or /stocks/trending
            {
                STOCK_ROUTES.map((route, index) => {
                    return (
                        <Route
                            key={index}
                            path={`${match.url}/${route.path}`}
                            component={route.component}
                        />
                    )
                })
            }
        </div>
    );
}
...
```

[38]

The route configuration defined in STOCK_ROUTES is used to add a list of `<Route>` components when the StockComponent renders. The parent `<Route>` component is rendered at the '/stocks' path, hence the use of match.url in the path when generating the `<Route>` component under the '/stocks' path.

Summary

In this chapter, we learned that the `<Route>` component can be configured using various props. This includes using the exact prop to render a component only when the browser's URL path matches the value mentioned in the `<Route>` component's path; using the strict prop in a `<Route>` component to ensure that the URL path matches the trailing slash mentioned in the path prop; including the sensitive prop to make the path prop value case-sensitive; and using the render and children props for inline rendering. The `<Route>` component with the children prop renders irrespective of the value specified in the path prop. This is useful in cases where you have several view components in the page layout and these should be rendered irrespective of the value specified in the path prop.

The component rendered as a result of the `<Route>` path match can receive data as props. This includes props such as history, location, match, and staticContext. The match prop can be used to used create nested routes, that is, the url property in the match prop contains information that can then be used in the path prop of the `<Route>` component included in the rendered component. The `<Route>` components can also be added by looking up the configuration specified in an object. An array containing path and component information can then be used to add multiple routes in the application.

The `<Route>` component's path prop can be configured to accept URL segments as path params. These params can then be read by the rendered component using match.params. The params can be configured to accept certain values by specifying a regular expression as a suffix to the path param.

3
Using the Link and NavLink Components to Navigate to a Route

React-Router provides the `<Link>` and `<NavLink>` components, which allow you to navigate to different routes defined in the application. These navigation components can be thought of as being like anchor links on the page that allow you to navigate to other pages in the site. In a traditional website, when you navigate through the application using anchor links, it results in a page refresh, and all the components in the page are re-rendered. Navigation links created with `<Link>` and `<NavLink>` do not result in a page refresh, and only those certain sections of the page that are defined using the `<Route>` and match the URL path are updated.

Similar to a `<Route>` component, the navigation components `<Link>` and `<NavLink>` are React components that allow you to define navigation links declaratively.

In this chapter, we will take a look at the various options available for navigating to routes defined in the application. This includes the following:

- The `<Link>` component and its props
- The `<NavLink>` component and its props
- Navigating to a nested route using the `match` prop
- Navigating to a route programmatically using `history`
- Using a High Order Component `withRouter`
- Preventing route transitions using the `<Prompt>` component

\<Link> component

A `<Link>` component is used to navigate to an `<indexentry content="component:about">` existing route that is defined using the `<Route>` component. To navigate to a route, specify the pathname used in the route as a value to the `to` prop:

```
import { Link } from 'react-router-dom';

class App extends Component {
    render() {
        return (
            <div class="container">
                <nav>
                    <Link to="/">Home</Link>
                    <Link to="/dashboard">Dashboard</Link>
                </nav>
                <Route
                    path="/"
                    component={HomeComponent}
                    exact
                />
                <Route
                    path="/dashboard"
                    component={DashboardComponent}
                />
            </div>
        );
    }
}
```

Notice that the `to` prop's value is the same as the value assigned to the `path` prop in `<Route>`. The page now renders two links:

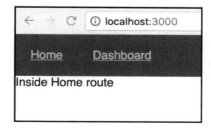

When you click on **Home**, you will see the text **Inside Home route** displayed, and, when you click on **Dashboard**, you will be navigated to the route with its `path` prop set to `/dashboard`.

When you navigate to a route using `<Link>`, `history.push()` is called, which adds an entry to the history stack. Thus, when you click the browser's back button, you will be navigated to the previous route that you were accessing (the **Home** route). As mentioned in the previous chapter, the `history` library is used by React-Router to maintain the state of the application as the user traverses through various routes during the application journey.

The `<Link>` component has two other props—`replace` and `innerRef`.

replace prop

The `replace` prop in `<Link>` calls `history.replace()`, which replaces the current entry in the history stack with the new path name mentioned in the `to` prop:

```
<Link to="/dashboard" replace>Dashboard</Link>
```

For example, if you access the page at the path `/home`, accessing the preceding link will replace the current entry in the history stack with `/dashboard`, which basically replaces the entry `/home` with `/dashboard`.

innerRef prop

React provides `ref` to get a reference to the rendered DOM element. This reference (`ref`) can then be used to perform certain operations outside the regular flow, such as focusing on the input element, media playback, and so on. `<Link>` is a composite component and it renders an anchor element on the DOM.

The `<Link>` component mentioned in the previous code snippet translates to anchor elements as follows:

```
..
<nav>
    <a href="/">Home</a>
    <a href="/dashboard">Dashboard</a>
</nav>
..
```

To get a reference to this rendered anchor element, the prop `innerRef` is added to `<Link>`:

```
<nav>
    <Link
        to="/"
        innerRef={this.refCallback}>
```

```
        Home
    </Link>
    <Link
        to="/dashboard"
        innerRef={this.refCallback}>
        Dashboard
    </Link>
</nav>
```

The `innerRef` prop accepts a callback function as its value; here, a function `refCallback` is specified as a value to the `innerRef` prop. The `refCallback` gets the reference to the inner element of the `<Link>` component:

```
refCallback(node) {
    node.onmouseover = () => {
        node.focus();
    }
}
```

The callback function—`refCallback`—is called when the `<Link>` component mounts. From the preceding code snippet, we can see that a `mouseover` handler is added for both the anchor elements rendered by the two `<Link>` components. When the user hovers over the link, the corresponding anchor gets a focus.

to prop with an object

The `to` prop can be either a string or an object. The object can contain the following properties:

- `pathname`: The path to navigate to
- `search`: The query parameters to the path, represented as a string value
- `hash`: a hash string to add to the URL
- `state`: an object containing state information that the rendered component can consume

Using these parameters, let's add a `<Link>` component:

```
<Link
    to={{
        pathname: '/user',
        search: '?id=1',
        hash: '#hash',
```

```
        state: { isAdmin: true }
    }}>
        User
</Link>
```

The preceding code translates to the following:

```
<a href="/user?id=1#hash">User</a>
```

The `state` information is not included in the URL path; however, it's available to the component that gets rendered as a result of a `<Route>` match:

```
<Route
    path="/user"
    render={({ location }) => {
        const { pathname, search, hash, state } = location;
        return (
            <div>
                Inside User route
                <h5>Pathname: {pathname}</h5>
                <h5>Search: {search}</h5>
                <h5>Hash: {hash}</h5>
                <h5>State: {'{'}
                    {Object.keys(state).map((element, index) => {
                        return (
                            <span key={index}>
                                {element}: {state[element].toString()}
                            </span>
                        )
                    })}
                    {'}'}
                </h5>
            </div>
        );
    }}
/>
```

The `location` object contains all of the previously defined parameters, including the `state` object.

The `state` object can be used to store data as the user navigates through the application and provide this data to the component that gets rendered next as a result of `<Route>` match.

<NavLink> component

The `<NavLink>` component is similar to the `<Link>` component, except that several props can be specified that help you to conditionally add styling attributes to the rendered element. It accepts the same set of props as the `<Link>` component (`to`, `replace`, and `innerRef`) for navigating to a route, and it includes props to style the selected route.

Let's take a look at these props that help you style the `<NavLink>` component.

activeClassName prop

By default, the class name `active` is applied to the active `<NavLink>` component. For example, when a `<NavLink>` is clicked and the corresponding route is rendered, the selected `<NavLink>` has its class name set to `active`. To change this class name, specify the `activeClassName` prop on the `<NavLink>` component with its value set as the CSS class name that you want to apply:

```
<nav>
    <NavLink to="/">Home</NavLink>
    <NavLink
        to="/dashboard"
        activeClassName="selectedLink">
        Dashboard
    </NavLink>
</nav>
```

The next step is to specify the styles for the CSS class `selectedLink` in your application's CSS file. Note that the first `<NavLink>` does not specify the `activeClassName` prop. In this case, when the `<NavLink>` is clicked, the `active` class is added:

```
<nav>
    <a class="active" aria-current="page" href="/">Home</a>
    <a aria-current="page" href="/dashboard">Dashboard</a>
</nav>
```

However, when the second `<NavLink>` is clicked, the `selectedLink` class is applied:

```
<nav>
    <a aria-current="page" href="/">Home</a>
    <a class="selectedLink" aria-current="page"
href="/dashboard">Dashboard</a>
</nav>
```

activeStyle prop

The `activeStyle` prop is also used to style the selected `<NavLink>`. However, instead of providing a class to apply when the `<NavLink>` is selected, the CSS style properties can be provided inline:

```
<NavLink
    to="/user"
    activeStyle={{
        background: 'red',
        color: 'white'
    }}>
    User
</NavLink>
```

exact prop

When you click on the `<NavLink>` with the `to` prop `/dashboard`, the `active` class (or inline style specified in `activeStyle` prop) is applied to both the `<NavLink>` components in the page. Similar to the `<Route>` component, the `/` in `/dashboard` matches the path specified in the `to` prop, and thus the active class is applied to both the `<NavLink>` components.

In this case, the `exact` prop can be used to apply the `active` class or `activeStyle` only when the path matches the browser's URL:

```
<NavLink
    to="/"
    exact>
    Home
</NavLink>
<NavLink
    to="/dashboard"
    activeClassName="selectedLink">
    Dashboard
</NavLink>
```

strict prop

The `<NavLink>` component also supports the `strict` prop, which can be used to match the trailing slash specified in the `to` prop:

```
<NavLink
    to="/dashboard/"
    activeClassName="selectedLink"
    strict>
    Dashboard
</NavLink>
```

Here, the class `selectedLink` is applied to the `<NavLink>` component only when the browser's URL path matches the path `/dashboard/`—for example, when a trailing slash is present in the URL.

isActive prop

The `isActive` prop is used to determine whether the `<NavLink>` component should have the `active` class applied (or inline styles specified in `activeStyle` prop). The function specified as a value to the `isActive` prop should return a Boolean value:

```
<NavLink
    to={{
        pathname: '/user',
        search: '?id=1',
        hash: '#hash',
        state: { isAdmin: true }
    }}
    activeStyle={{
        background: 'red',
        color: 'white'
    }}
    isActive={(match, location) => {
        if (!match) {
            return false;
        }
        const searchParams = new URLSearchParams(location.search);
        return match.isExact && searchParams.has('id');
    }}>
    User
</NavLink>
```

From the preceding example, the function accepts two parameters—`match` and `location`. The styles defined in the `activeStyle` prop are applied only when the condition `match.isExact && searchParams.has('id')` evaluates to true, so, only when the `match` is `exact` and the URL has a query parameter `id`.

When the browser's URL is `/user`, the corresponding route defined with `<Route>` is displayed. However, the `<NavLink>` component will have the default styling and not the styles mentioned in the `activeStyle` prop, since the query parameter `id` is missing.

location prop

The `isActive` function in `<NavLink>` receives the browser's history `location` and determines whether the browser's `location.pathname` matches the given condition. To provide a different location, include the `location` prop:

```
<NavLink
    to="/user"
    activeStyle={{
        background: 'red',
        color: 'white'
    }}
    location={{
        search: '?id=2',
    }}
    isActive={(match, location) => {
        if (!match) {
            return false;
        }
        const searchParams = new URLSearchParams(location.search);
        return match.isExact && searchParams.has('id');
    }}>
    User
</NavLink>
```

Notice that the `to` prop doesn't specify the `search` parameter; however, the `location` prop includes it, and thus, when the browser's location is `/user`, the `isActive` function returns true, since the search parameter includes the `id` property.

Navigating to nested routes

In the last chapter, we saw how to create nested routes using the `match` prop that the rendered component receives. The `match.url` property contains the browser's URL path that matched the `<Route>` component's path. Similarly, the `<Link>` and `<NavLink>` components can be used to create navigation links to access these nested routes:

```
<nav>
    <Link
        to={`${match.url}/pictures`}>
        Pictures
    </Link>
    <NavLink
        to={`${match.url}/books`}
        activeStyle={{
            background: 'orange'
        }}>
     Books
    </NavLink>
</nav>
```

In the preceding code snippet, the `<Link>` and `<NavLink>` components make use of `match.url` to get a reference to the current rendered route and add the additional path values required to navigate to the nested route.

Navigating to a route programmatically using history

The `<Link>` and `<NavLink>` components render anchor links on the page, which allow you to navigate from the current route to the new route. However, in many cases, the user should be navigated to a new route programmatically when an event occurs. For example, the user should be navigated to a new route upon clicking the **Submit** button in the login form. The `history` object available to the rendered component can be used in such cases:

```
export const DashboardComponent = (props) => (
    <div className="dashboard">
        Inside Dashboard route
        <button onClick={() => props.history.push('/user')}>
            User
        </button>
    </div>
);
```

[50]

Here, the `DashboardComponent` receives `props` as its argument, which contains the `history` object. The `onClick` handler calls `props.history.push` with the pathname `/user`. This call adds an entry to the history stack, and navigates the user to the `<Route>` with the path `/user`. The `history` object can also be used to replace the current entry in the history stack by using `history.replace` in place of `history.push`.

Using the withRouter higher-order component

The `history` object is available to the component rendered with a `<Route>` match. In the preceding example, the `DashboardComponent` was rendered as a result of navigation to the path `/dashboard`. The rendered component received the `props`, which contained the `history` object (as well as `match`, `location`, and `staticContext`). In a case where, the rendered component on the page is not the outcome of a route navigation, the `history` object will not be available to the component.

Consider a `FooterComponent` included in `App.js`:

```
class FooterComponent extends Component {
    render() {
        return (
            <footer>
                In Footer
                <div>
                    <button
                        onClick={() =>
                        this.props.history.push('/user')}>
                        User
                    </button>
                    <button
                        onClick={() =>
                         this.props.history.push('/stocks')}>
                        Stocks
                    </button>
                </div>
            </footer>
        )
    }
}
```

Using the Link and NavLink Components to Navigate to a Route

The `FooterComponent` has two buttons that call `history.push` to navigate to one of the pages in the application. On clicking the button, the error `TypeError: Cannot read property 'push' of undefined` is thrown. The error is thrown because the `history` object is not available in the `props` property, as the component is not rendered as a result of navigation. To circumvent this, use the higher-order component `withRouter`:

```
export const Footer = withRouter(FooterComponent);
```

Here, the `withRouter` function defined in the `react-router` package accepts a React component as its argument and augments it to provide the necessary objects on the `props` property—`history`, `match`, `location`, and `staticContext`.

React documentation on HOC: A higher-order component is a function that takes a component and returns a new component. Although a component transforms props into UI, a higher-order component transforms a component into another component.

A component wrapped inside a `withRouter` HOC can define routes and navigation links using `<Route>`, `<Link>`, and `<NavLink>`:

```
import { withRouter } from 'react-router';

class FooterComponent extends Component {
    render() {
        return (
            <footer>
                In Footer
                <div>
                <button onClick={() =>
                 this.props.history.push('/user')}>User</button>
                <button onClick={() =>
                 this.props.history.push('/stocks')}>Stocks</button>
                <Link to='subroute'>User</Link>
                <Route
                    path='/subroute'
                    render={() => {
                        return <span>Inside Footer Subroute</span>
                    }} />
                </div>
            </footer >
        )
    }
}

export const Footer = withRouter(FooterComponent);
```

In the preceding code snippet, the `withRouter` HOC enables the component to get the context of the router, and hence makes components such as `Link`, `NavLink`, and `Route` available.

Preventing transitions with <Prompt>

When you navigate between the pages in the application, the transition to the new route occurs instantly. However, there are scenarios in which you want to prevent this transition based on the state of the application. One such common example is when a user has entered data into form fields and has spent several minutes (or hours) filling up the form data. If the user clicks on a navigation link accidentally, all the data entered in the form will be lost. The user should be notified of this route navigation, so that the user gets a chance to save the data entered into the form.

Traditional websites keep track of the state of the form and display a confirmation message when the user tries to navigate away from a page that contains a form that has not been submitted to the server. In these scenarios, a confirmation dialog box is shown with two options, **OK** and **CANCEL**; the former option allows the user to transition to the next step and the latter cancels the transition:

React-Router provides the `<Prompt>` component, which can be used to display a confirmation dialog box to prevent the user from navigating away from the current `<Route>` accidentally:

```
import { Prompt } from 'react-router-dom'

<Prompt
    when={this.state.isFormSubmitted}
    message='Are you sure?'
/>
```

The `<Prompt>` component here accepts two props—`when` and `message`. From the preceding code snippet, it can be seen that a confirmation dialog box with the message **Are you sure?** is shown to the user if the value of the `state` property `isFormSubmitted` is `true`, and when the user tries to navigate away from the current route.

> Please note, the `<Prompt>` message is shown only when the user tries to navigate away from the current route. No message is shown when the `state` property is set to `true`.

The value assigned to the `when` prop can be any Boolean variable or a Boolean value. In React, the component's `state` is used as a View-Model to maintain the state of the rendered component. The `state` properties are ideal in cases such as these to determine whether the `<Prompt>` should be shown when the user tries to navigate away from the current route.

The value of the `message` prop can be a string or a function:

```
<Prompt
    when={this.state.isFormSubmitted}
    message={(location) => 'Are you sure you want to navigate to ${location.pathname}?'} />
```

The function receives the `location` parameter, which includes the location information about the route that the user is trying to navigate to.

> Similar to other components in the `'react-router-dom'` package, the `<Prompt>` component should be used inside a rendered `<Route>`. When you try to use a `<Prompt>` without it having the context of the current route, the message. You should not use `<Prompt>` outside a `<Router>` is shown.

It's also possible to show a message whenever the user tries to navigate away from the current route (irrespective of the `state` of the application) by not including the `when` prop:

```
<Prompt message='Are you sure?' />
```

More often than not, the `when` prop is included in `<Prompt>`, and the value assigned to the `when` prop is used to determine whether the confirmation dialog box should be shown.

> When you're trying these examples, ensure that you have only one `<Prompt>` for the given `<Route>`, else the library will report the warning `A history supports only one prompt at a time`.

[54]

Summary

In this chapter, we looked at how the `<Link>` and `<NavLink>` navigation components can be used to navigate to various routes defined in the application. These components render `anchor` links in the page, and, when the user clicks on these links, sections of the page are updated as opposed to doing a complete page reload, thus providing a lucid user experience. The `<Link>` component accepts the props `to`, `replace`, and `innerRef`.

The `<NavLink>` component is similar to the `<Link>` component, and it accepts all the props that the `<Link>` component works with. In addition to adding a link to the page, the `<NavLink>` component accepts several props—`activeClassName`, `activeStyle`, `exact`, `strict`, and `isActive`.

To create links to the nested routes, the `<Link>` and `<NavLink>` components can use the prefix `match.url` in the `to` prop. Also, you can programmatically navigate using `history.push` or `history.replace` in the event-handler function. Props—`history`, `match`, `location`, and `staticContext`—can be made available to components rendered outside the Route context via the `withRouter` higher order component. The `'react-router-dom'` package includes a `<Prompt>` component that can be used to display a confirmation dialog box when the user tries to navigate to route by accidentally clicking on a navigation link. The `<Prompt>` component accepts the `when` and `message` prop, and, based on the Boolean value assigned to the `when` prop, the message specified in the `message` prop will be shown to the user.

In `Chapter 4`, *Using the Redirect and Switch Components*, we will take a look at the `<Redirect>` and `<Switch>` components. Also, we will see how these components can be used to protect the routes and display a Page Not Found page when none of the routes in the page match the requested URL.

4
Using the Redirect and Switch Components

Redirecting the user from one route to the other can be achieved using React-Router's `<Redirect>` component. In traditional websites, where pages are rendered on the server side, the web server hosting the application is configured with rewrite rules that redirect the user to a different URL. This redirection could be used when the content has moved to a new page, and in cases where certain pages of the site are still under construction. HTTP redirection is an expensive operation and thus the application's performance is also affected.

In **single–page application (SPA)**, the redirection occurs on the browser, where the user is redirected to a different route based on a certain condition. This redirection is faster, since there's no HTTP roundtrip involved, and the transition is similar to navigating from one route to the other using the `<Link>` or `<NavLink>` components.

In this chapter, the following topics are discussed:

- `<Redirect>` component: Redirecting the user from one route to the other route
- Protecting routes and authorization: A use case where the user is redirected to the login page when an attempt is made to access a protected route
- `<Switch>` component: Rendering the first matching `<Route>`
- Adding a 404 Page Not Found page: A use case where `<Switch>` and `<Route>` or `<Switch>` and `<Redirect>` components are used to render a 404 page when none of the `<Route>` components match the browser's URL path

The <Redirect> component

The `<Redirect>` component is included in the `react-router-dom` package. It helps in redirecting the user from the component where it's included to the route specified in the `'to'` prop:

```
import { Redirect } from 'react-router-dom';

export class HomeComponent extends Component {
    render() {
        return (
            <Redirect to='/dashboard' />
        )
    }
}
```

In the preceding scenario, when `HomeComponent` is rendered (based on a `<Route>` match), the user is redirected to the `'/dashboard'` route. For example, when the user accesses the home page (at path `'/'`), the `<Route>` with the path `'/'` renders the previous component and then the user is immediately redirected to the `<Route>` with its path value as `'/dashboard'`. This is similar to how a `<Link>` or `<NavLink>` component with a `'to'` prop is used to navigate the user to a different route. Here, instead of triggering the navigation as a result of a user action, the redirection happens when the component is rendered.

The redirection example mentioned previously is ideal in scenarios where certain pages in the application have moved to a different directory.

The `<Redirect>` component is similar to other components in React-Router, such as `<Route>` and `<Link>`. As observed previously, it's a React component that can be included in the render function. Also, the `<Redirect>` component accepts a similar set of props to the `<Link>` component.

The to prop

The to prop is used to specify the route to which the user should be redirected. If a matching `<Route>` is found, the user is redirected to the specified path and the corresponding component is rendered.

The to prop can also accept an object that specifies the values for the pathname, search, hash, and state properties:

```
<Redirect
    to={{
        pathname: '/dashboard',
        search: '?q=1',
        hash: '#hash',
        state: { from: match.url }
    }}
/>
```

Similar to the <Link> component, the previously mentioned properties are specified in the to prop of the <Redirect> component. Notice that the state property has the value { from: match.url }. Here, match.url provides the current value of the browser's URL path and this value is then provided to the rendered component when the redirection occurs.

The rendered component can then read the state information using this.props.location.state:

```
export class DashboardComponent extends Component {
    render() {
        const { location } = this.props;
        return (
            <div>
                In DashboardComponent <br />
                From : {location.state.from}
            </div>
        )
    }
}
```

In the preceding example, DashboardComponent is rendered as a result of a redirection from the HomeComponent. The value of location.state.from shares the path information to the redirected component about the page from which the redirection occurred. This is useful when you have a generic page to which you want to be redirected and the redirected page has to display information about the path from which the redirection occurred. For example, when an error occurs in the application, the user should be redirected to a page that renders the error message, providing information on the page where the error occurred. In this case, the state information could include properties—errorMessage and from; the latter's value as match.url that is the page where the error occurred.

If the redirected <Route> is not found, the browser's URL is updated and no errors are thrown. This is by design; ideally, if there is no matching route, the user should be redirected to a 404 or a Page Not Found page. The <Route> to render when there's no match is discussed in the next section.

Inside the component, when you try to redirect to the same route, React-Router throws a warning message **Warning: You tried to redirect to the same route you're currently on:** "/home". This check ensures that the redirect does not lead to an infinite loop.

It's also possible to run into a situation where the redirected component includes a <Redirect> in its render method, redirecting back to the same route, that is, following this route redirect path: /home => /dashboard => /home. This runs into a loop until React stops rendering the component; React then throws an error Maximum update depth exceeded. This can happen when a component repeatedly calls setState inside componentWillUpdate or componentDidUpdate. React limits the number of nested updates to prevent infinite loops. React-Router uses state to keep track of the user's location in the application journey and thus the preceding error occurs when React tries to update the state several times because of redirection. When working with redirection, you need to ensure that it does not lead to an infinite loop of redirection.

The push prop

The <Redirect> component redirects the user to the given path by calling history.replace(<path>), that is, replacing the current entry in the history stack with the new path. By specifying the push prop in the <Redirect> component, history.push is called instead of history.replace:

```
<Redirect to="/dashboard" push />
```

Protecting routes and authorization

The routes defined using the `<Route>` component can be accessed through the browser's URL, by navigating to the route using `<Link>` or `<NavLink>`, or by redirecting the user with the `<Redirect>` component. However, in most applications, some of the routes should be accessible only to authorized or logged-in users. For example, say the `/user` path displays the logged-in user's data; this path should be protected and only the logged-in user should be allowed to access the route. In these cases, the `<Redirect>` component comes in handy for redirecting the user to the login page (at the path `/login`) when you try to access the path `/user`.

To demonstrate this, let's create a component called `UserComponent`, which will be rendered when you try to access the path `/user`:

```
export class UserComponent extends Component {
    render() {
        const { location } = this.props;
        return (
            <div>
                Username: {location && location.state ? location.state.userName
                    : ''} <br />
                From: {location && location.state ? location.state.from :
''}
                 <br />
                <button onClick={this.logout}>LOGOUT</button>
            </div>
        )
    }
}
```

From the preceding code snippet, we can see that `UserComponent` displays state information available in `this.props.location` and the **LOGOUT** button.

To check whether the user has logged in, a request to the server should be made to check if the user's session exists. However, in our case, a check to see if the user is logged in would be made by referring to a variable in the browser's `localStorage`:

```
export class UserComponent extends Component {
    state = {
        isUserLoggedIn: false
    }
    componentWillMount() {
        const isUserLoggedIn = localStorage.getItem('isUserLoggedIn');
        this.setState({isUserLoggedIn});
    }
    render() {
        ...
    }
}
```

Here, the component's state property, `isUserLoggedIn`, will be updated with the value stored in the localStorage variable of the same name.

The next step is to use this state information in the render function of the `UserComponent` class and redirect the user using the `<Redirect>` component:

```
export class UserComponent extends Component {
    ...
    render() {
        const { location } = this.props;
        if (!this.state.isUserLoggedIn) {
            return (
                <Redirect to="/login" />
            );
        }
        ...
    }
}
```

Here, the value of the state property, `isUserLoggedIn`, is checked, and, if it evaluates to false, or if it's not found, then the user is redirected to the route with the path `'/login'`.

The last step would be to implement the `logout` function, which is called when the user clicks the **LOGOUT** button:

```
export class UserComponent extends Component {
    logout = (event) => {
        localStorage.removeItem('isUserLoggedIn');
        this.setState({ isUserLoggedIn: false });
    }
    ...
}
```

Logging the user out involves removing the `localStorage` variable and updating the state property `isUserLoggedIn` to `'false'`.

With these changes, when the state property—`isUserLoggedIn`—is set to false, the `UserComponent` is rerendered and the user is redirected to the path `/login`, asking the user to provide credentials to access the page. Also, now when you try to access the path `/user` by the entering the same in the browser's address bar, the `<Route>` with its path prop `/user` would match. However, when `UserComponent` is rendered, the state property `isUserLoggedIn` would evaluate to false, redirecting the user to the `/login` page.

Redirecting with a callback route

When you try to access a protected `<Route>`, you will be redirected to the login page to provide credentials. After providing credentials, you should be redirected to the page that you tried to access earlier. For example, when you try to access the protected route at the path `/stocks`, you would be redirected to the path `/login`, and then, on providing correct credentials, you should be redirected to the same path `/stocks` that you tried to access earlier. However, from the previous example, you would be redirected to the path `/user` and the user's profile information would be displayed. The desired behavior is to be redirected to the protected route `/stocks` instead of the path `/user`.

This can be accomplished by providing state information when redirecting the user.

In `StocksComponent` (a component rendered as a result of a `<Route>` match, `/stocks`), when you redirect the user to the login page, provide the state information in the to prop:

```
export class StocksComponent extends Component {
    ...
    render() {
        const {match} = this.props;
        if (!this.state.isUserLoggedIn) {
            return (
```

Using the Redirect and Switch Components

```
                <Redirect
                    to={{
                        pathname: "/login",
                        state: { callbackURL: match.url }
                    }}
                />
            )
        }

        return (
            <div>
                In StocksComponent
            </div>
        )
    }
}
```

In the component's render function, the user is redirected to the login page using the `<Redirect>` component. The `<Redirect>` component here includes a to prop specifying the `pathname` to which the user should be redirected, and it also includes a state object mentioning the `callbackURL` property. The value of the `callbackURL` property is `match.url`, that is, the current browser URL path `/stocks`.

This state information can then be used in the `LoginComponent` to redirect the user to the path `/stocks`:

```
export class LoginComponent extends Component {
    ...
    render() {
        const { location: { state } } = this.props;
        if (this.state.isUserLoggedIn) {
            return (
                <Redirect
                    to={{
                        pathname: state &&
                        state.callbackURL || "/user",
                        state: {
                            from: this.props.match.url,
                            userName: this.state.userName
                        }
                    }}
                />
            )
        }
        ...
    }
}
```

Here, when the user provides credentials to access the protected route, the `<Redirect>` component redirects the user to the path mentioned in the `state.callbackURL`. If `callbackURL` is not available, the user would be redirected to the default route, which is redirected to the path `/user`.

A combination of Route component props, `match.url`, and location.state can be used to redirect the user to the protected route that was requested earlier.

Exclusive routing with the <Switch> component

When a URL is presented to `<BrowserRouter>`, it will look for routes created with `<Route>` components and render all the routes that match the browser's URL path. For example, consider the following routes:

```
<Route
    path="/login"
    component={LoginComponent}
/>
<Route
    path="/:id"
    render={({ match }) =>
        <div> Route with path {match.url}</div>
    }
/>
```

Here, both the routes with the paths `/login` and `/:id` match the `/login` URL path. React-Router renders all the `<Route>` components that match the URL path. However, to render only the first matching route, the library provides the `<Switch>` component. The `<Switch>` component accepts a list of `<Route>` components as its children and it renders only the first `<Route>` that matches the browser's URL:

```
<Switch>
    <Route
        path="/login"
        component={LoginComponent}
    />
    <Route
        path="/:id"
```

Using the Redirect and Switch Components

```
            render={({ match }) =>
                <div> Route with path {match.url}</div>
            }
        />
</Switch>
```

By wrapping a list of <Route> components inside a <Switch> component, React-Router sequentially searches for a <Route> matching the browser's URL path. Once a matching <Route> is found, <Switch> stops the search and renders the matching <Route>.

In the preceding example, the first <Route> in <Switch> is rendered only if the browser's URL path is /login and paths other than /login (/123, /products, /stocks and so on) would match the second route and render the corresponding component.

If the order of the previous two <Route> components is swapped (that is, the <Route> with path /:id is listed above the <Route> with path /login), the <Route> with path /login would never get rendered because <Switch> allows only one and the first matching route to be rendered.

Ordering of the <Route> components in <Switch>

The ordering of the `<Route>` components inside `<Switch>` matters because the `<Switch>` component looks for a matching `<Route>` sequentially, and once a `<Route>` matching the browser's URL is found, it stops the search. This behavior may not be desired and you may want to render another route listed inside `<Switch>`. However, it can be corrected by changing the order in which `<Route>` are listed in `<Switch>`:

In the following examples, some of the common mistakes in listing the <Route> components in `<Switch>` are mentioned:

<Route> with path '/' as the first child in <Switch>

Consider the following code snippet:

```
<Switch>
    <Route
        path="/"
        component={LoginComponent}
    />
    <Route
        path="/dashboard"
        component={DashboardComponent}
    />
</Switch>
```

If the browser's URL path is `/dashboard`, it would match the first `<Route>` with path `/` and the `<Route>` with path `/dashboard` would never be matched and rendered. To fix this, either include the exact prop or list the `<Route>` with path `/` as the last entry in `<Switch>`.

`<Route>` with path params

In the following code snippet, a `<Route>` with a path param is listed as the second entry:

```
<Switch>
    <Route
        path="/github"
        component={LoginComponent}
    />
    <Route
        path="/github/:userId"
        component={DashboardComponent}
    />
</Switch>
```

In the previous example, `<Route>` with path `/github` would match the URL path `/github` as well as path `/github/mjackson`; thus, the first `<Route>` is rendered even when a `<Route>` with a specific path is available. To fix this, either provide the exact prop or list the `<Route>` with path `/github` below the `<Route>` with path `/github/:userId`.

From both cases mentioned in the previous paragraph, listing `<Route>` components with specific paths above `<Route>` components with generic paths would avoid undesirable results.

Adding a 404 – Page Not Found

As mentioned, the `<Switch>` component looks through all the `<Route>` components sequentially for a match and stops the search once a `<Route>` with its path matching the browser's URL is found. This is unlike a list `<Route>` in a page, where every matched `<Route>` is rendered. The `<Switch>` thus becomes a good fit for rendering a `Page Not Found` page, that is, rendering a component when none of the `<Route>` mentioned as children to `<Switch>` match the browser's URL.

Using the Redirect and Switch Components

Let's include a `<Route>` with no path prop as the last entry in `<Switch>`:

```
<Switch>
    <Route
        path="/login"
        component={LoginComponent}
    />
    <Route
        path="/user"
        render={({ match }) =>
            <div> Route with path {match.url}</div>
        }
    />
    <Route
        render={({ location }) =>
            <div> 404 - {location.pathname} not
            found</div>
        }
    />
</Switch>
```

From the preceding code snippet, we can see that when none of the `<Route>` with a path prop match the browser's URL, the last `<Route>` without the path prop would match and render.

It's important to include the `Page Not Found` `<Route>` as the last entry because the `<Switch>` component stops the search once a matching `<Route>` is found. In the preceding case, if the `<Route>` with no prop is included above other `<Route>`, then the `Page Not Found` route would be rendered even if a `<Route>` matching the browser's URL was present in the list.

You could also specify a `<Route>` with its path prop value as * instead of `<Route>` with no path prop, to render a `Page Not Found` page:

```
<Switch>
    ...
    <Route
        path="*"
        render={({ location }) =>
            <div> 404 - {location.pathname} not
            found</div>
        }
    />
</Switch>
```

[68]

In both cases, the path would match the browser's URL and render the Page Not Found page.

Using <Redirect> in <Switch> to redirect to a Page Not Found page

The `<Switch>` component's children can include a list of `<Route>` and `<Redirect>` components as well. The `<Redirect>` component, when included as the last entry in `<Switch>`, will redirect the user to the given path if none of the `<Route>` mentioned above the `<Redirect>` component match the browser's URL:

```
<Switch>
    <Route
        path="/login"
        component={LoginComponent}
    />
    <Route
        path="/user"
        render={({ match }) =>
            <div> Route with path {match.url}</div>
        }
    />
    <Redirect to="/home" />
</Switch>
```

The `<Redirect>` component mentioned previously redirects the user to the `<Route>` with path `/home`. This is similar to displaying a `404: Page Not Found page`; instead of displaying the component in line, the user is redirected to a different route.

For example, if the browser's URL path is `/dashboard`, the first two routes (with the paths `/login` and `/user`) wouldn't match, and thus the user is redirected using the `<Redirect>` component mentioned as the last entry in `<Switch>`.

Redirecting from an old path to a new path

The `<Redirect>` component can also be used to redirect the user from a given path to a new path. The `<Redirect>` component accepts a prop, from, which can be used to specify the path that should match the browser's URL from which the user should be redirected. Also, the path that the user should be redirected to should be specified in the to prop:

```
<Switch>
    <Route
        path="/login"
        component={LoginComponent}
    />
    <Route
        path="/user"
        render={(({ match }) =>
            <div> Route with path {match.url}</div>
        }
    />
    <Redirect
        from="/home"
        to="/login"
    />
    <Redirect to="/home" />
</Switch>
```

From the preceding example, we can see that when the browser's URL path is /home, the `<Redirect>` component with the from prop would match the given path and redirect the user to the `<Route>` with the path /login.

The `<Redirect>` component's from prop is useful when some of the pages on the site have been moved to a new directory. For example, if the user page has been moved to a new directory path, settings/user, then `<Redirect from="/user" to="/settings/user" />` will redirect the user to the new path.

Summary

The `<Redirect>` component can be used to redirect the user from the current rendered route to a new route. The component accepts props: to and push. This redirection could be used when the components in the application have moved to a different directory, or when the user is not authorized to visit the page. The `<Redirect>` component is helpful when a user visits a protected route and only authorized users are allowed to view the page.

The `<Switch>` component is used when only one `<Route>` out of a list of `<Route>` should be rendered. The `<Switch>` component accepts a list of `<Route>` and `<Redirect>` components as its children, and sequentially searches for a matching `<Route>` or a `<Redirect>` component. When a match is found, `<Switch>` renders the component and stops looking for a matching path.

This behavior of `<Switch>` can be leveraged to build a `404: Page Not Found`, which would be rendered when none of the `<Route>` components listed in `<Switch>` match the browser's URL path. By listing a `<Route>` without any path prop as the last entry in `<Switch>`, the `<Route>` is rendered if none of the `<Route>` components listed above match the browser's URL path. Alternatively, the `<Redirect>` component can be listed as the last entry to redirect the user to a page when none of the `<Route>` components in the `<Switch>` match.

5
Understanding the Core Router, and Configuring the BrowserRouter and HashRouter components

The React-Router library provides several components that address various use cases, such as adding navigation links with `<Link>` and `<NavLink>`, redirecting the user using the `<Redirect>` component, and so on. The `<BrowserRouter>` component wraps the application's root component (`<App />`) and enables these components to interact with the `history` object. When the application initializes, the `<BrowserRouter>` component initializes the `history` object and makes it available to all its child components using React's `context`.

Routing in a single-page application is not really routing; rather, it's conditional rendering of components. The `<BrowserRouter>` component creates the `history` object, and the `history` object has methods such as `push`, `replace`, `pop`, and so on, which are used when navigation occurs. The `history` object enables the application to maintain history when the user is navigating between the pages. Other than `<BrowserRouter>`, React-Router provides various Router implementations—`<HashRouter>`, `<StaticRouter>`, `<MemoryRouter>`, and `<NativeRouter>`. These Routers make use of the low-level `Router` interface, which is included in the `react-router` core package.

In this chapter, we will take a look at the low-level `<Router>` component and various router implementations:

- `<Router>` and the `react-router` package
- `<BrowserRouter>` props
- `HashRouter`—a Router implementation for use in legacy browsers

Other `<Router>` implementations, such as `<StaticRouter>`, `<MemoryRouter>`, and `<NativeRouter>`, are discussed in the next chapters.

`<Router>` component

As previously mentioned, React-Router provides various Router implementations:

- `<BrowserRouter>`
- `<HashRouter>`
- `<MemoryRouter>`
- `<StaticRouter>`
- `<NativeRouter>`

These Routers make use of a low-level interface—`<Router>`. The `<Router>` component is part of the core `react-router` package, and the functionality provided by the `<Router>` interface is extended by these Router implementations.

The `<Router>` component accepts two props—`history` and `children`. The `history` object can be a reference to the browser's history or it can be the application's history maintained in memory (which is useful in native applications where an instance of browser's history is not available). The `<Router>` component accepts one child component, which is generally the application's root component. Also, it creates a `context` object, `context.router`, through which all its descendent child components, such as `<Route>`, `<Link>`, `<Switch>`, and so on, get a reference for the `history` object.

From reactjs.org:

> *Context provides a way to pass data through the component tree without having to pass props down manually at every level.*

The `<Router>` interface is generally not used in building applications; instead, one of the high-level Router components that is suitable for the given environment is used. One of the common use cases for using the `<Router>` interface is to synchronize a custom `history` object with state-management libraries such as `Redux` and `MobX`.

Including <Router> from react-router

The core `react-router` package can be installed via `npm`:

```
npm install --save react-router
```

The `Router` class can then be included in the application file:

```
import { Router } from 'react-router'
```

The next step is to create a `history` object that can then be provided as a value to the `history` prop of `<Router>`:

```
import createBrowserHistory from 'history/createBrowserHistory';

const customHistory = createBrowserHistory()
```

Here, the `createBrowserHistory` class from the `history` package is used to create a `history` object for the browser environment. The `history` package includes classes suitable for various environments.

The last step is to wrap the application's root component with the `<Router>` component and render the application:

```
ReactDOM.render(
    <Router history={customHistory}>
        <App />
    </Router>, document.getElementById('root'));
```

Notice that the `<Router>` component accepts a `history` prop whose value is the `history` object created with `createBrowserHistory`. Similar to the `<BrowserRouter>` component, the `<Router>` component accepts only one child, and throws an error when there is more than one child component.

React allows its prop values to change and it re-renders the component whenever a change is detected. In this case, if we try to change the value assigned to the history prop, React-Router throws a warning message. Consider the following code snippet:

```
class App extends Component {
    state = {
        customHistory: createBrowserHistory()
    }

    componentDidMount() {
        this.setState({
            customHistory: createBrowserHistory()
        });
    }

    render() {
        return (
            <Router history={this.state.customHistory}>
                <Route
                    path="/"
                    render={() => <div> In Home </div>}
                />
            </Router>
        );
    }
}
```

In the preceding example, the state property `customHistory` contains the `history` object, which is provided to the `<Router>` component. However, when the value of `customHistory` changes in the `componentDidMount` lifecycle function, React-Router throws the warning message **Warning: You cannot change <Router> history**.

react-router package

The `react-router` package includes some of the core components, such as the `<Router>` component mentioned previously. The package also includes several other components that are then used by components available in the `react-router-dom` and `react-router-native` packages. The `react-router` package exports these components:

```
export MemoryRouter from "./MemoryRouter";
export Prompt from "./Prompt";
export Redirect from "./Redirect";
export Route from "./Route";
export Router from "./Router";
export StaticRouter from "./StaticRouter";
```

```
export Switch from "./Switch";
export generatePath from "./generatePath";
export matchPath from "./matchPath";
export withRouter from "./withRouter";
```

Some of the components mentioned here were discussed in earlier chapters. The package also provides helper functions, such as `generatePath` and `matchPath`, and router implementations, such as `<MemoryRouter>` and `<StaticRouter>`. The components and services defined in `react-router-dom` and `react-router-native` import these components and services, and are included in their respective packages.

react-router-dom package

The `react-router-dom` package provides components that can be used in a browser-based application. It declares a dependency on the `react-router` package and exports the following components:

```
export BrowserRouter from "./BrowserRouter";
export HashRouter from "./HashRouter";
export Link from "./Link";
export MemoryRouter from "./MemoryRouter";
export NavLink from "./NavLink";
export Prompt from "./Prompt";
export Redirect from "./Redirect";
export Route from "./Route";
export Router from "./Router";
export StaticRouter from "./StaticRouter";
export Switch from "./Switch";
export generatePath from "./generatePath";
export matchPath from "./matchPath";
export withRouter from "./withRouter";
```

Notice that some of the components mentioned here are also included in the `react-router` package. The components in `react-router-dom` import the components defined in `react-router` and then export them. For example, take a look at the `<Route>` component:

```
import { Route } from "react-router";
export default Route;
```

The Router implementations `BrowserRouter`, `<HashRouter>`, and `<MemoryRouter>` create a `history` object specific to the given environment, and render the `<Router>` component. We will take a look at these Router implementations shortly.

Understanding the Core Router, and Configuring the BrowserRouter and HashRouter components

The `react-router-native` package makes use of the `<MemoryRouter>` implementation in `react-router`, and provides a `<NativeRouter>` interface. The `NativeRouter` implementation and its packaging details are discussed in upcoming chapters.

`<BrowserRouter>` component

The `<BrowserRouter>` component was discussed briefly in the first chapter. As the name suggests, the `<BrowserRouter>` component is used in browser-based applications and it uses HTML5's history API to keep the UI in sync with the browser's URL. Here, we take a look at how the component creates a `history` object for the browser environment and provides this `history` object to the `<Router>`.

The `<BrowserRouter>` component accepts the following props:

```
static propTypes = {
    basename: PropTypes.string,
    forceRefresh: PropTypes.bool,
    getUserConfirmation: PropTypes.func,
    keyLength: PropTypes.number,
    children: PropTypes.node
};
```

Similar to the `<Router>` interface, the `<BrowserRouter>` accepts only one child component (usually the application's root component). The `children` prop mentioned in the preceding code snippet refers to this child node. The `createBrowserHistory` method from the `history` package is used to create a `history` object for initializing the `<Router>`:

```
import { createBrowserHistory as createHistory } from "history";
import Router from "./Router";

class BrowserRouter extends React.Component {
    ...
    history = createHistory(this.props);
    ...
    render() {
        return <Router
                    history={this.history}
                    children={this.props.children}
                />;
    }
}
```

In the preceding code snippet, the `<BrowserRouter>` uses the provided props to create a `history` object using the `history/createBrowserHistory` class. The component then renders the `<Router>` component, and provides the created `history` object and the `children` object from props.

basename prop

The `basename` prop is used to provide a base URL path for all the locations in the application. For example, if you want to render your application at the `/admin` path instead of rendering at the root path `/`, then specify the `basename` prop in `<BrowserRouter>`:

```
<BrowserRouter basename="/admin">
    <App />
</BrowerRouter>
```

The `basename` prop now adds the base URL path `/admin` to the application. When you navigate using `<Link>` and `<NavLink>`, the `basename` path is added to the URL. For example, consider the following code with two `<Link>` components:

```
<BrowserRouter basename="/admin">
    <div className="component">
        <nav>
            <Link to="/">Home</Link>
            <Link to="/dashboard">Dashboard</Link>
        </nav>
    </div>
</BrowserRouter>
```

When you click on the `Home` link (path `/`), you'll notice that the URL path is updated to `/admin` instead of `/`. And, when you click on the `Dashboard` link, the updated URL path is `/admin/dashboard`. With the `basename` prop in `<BrowserRouter>`, the preceding `<Link>` components translate to the following:

```
<a href='/admin'>Home</a>
<a href='/admin/dashboard'>Dashboard</a>
```

The anchor link's `href` attribute is prefixed with the `/admin` path.

forceRefresh prop

The `forceRefresh` prop is a Boolean prop, and when set to `true`, navigation to any route will result in a page refresh—instead of updating specific sections of the page, the entire page is reloaded:

```
<BrowserRouter forceRefresh={true}>
    <Link to="/dashboard">Dashboard</Link>
</BrowserRouter>
```

When you click on the navigation link `Dashboard`, you'll notice that the page reloads when requesting for the URL path `/dashboard`.

keyLengthprop

The `keyLength` prop is used to specify the length for the `location.key`. The `locaction.key` property represents a unique key that is provided to a location. Take a look at the following code snippet:

```
<BrowserRouter keyLength={10}>
    <div className="container">
        <nav>
            <Link to="/dashboard">Dashboard</Link>
            <Link to="/user">User</Link>
        </nav>
        <Route
            path="/dashboard"
            render={({ location }) =>
                <div> In Dashboard, Location Key: {location.key} </div>
            }
        />
        <Route
            path="/user"
            render={({ location }) =>
                <div> In User, Location Key: {location.key} </div>
            }
        />
    </div>
</BrowserRouter>
```

When you navigate to either of the `/dashboard` or `/user` paths, the value of `location.key` will be a random alphanumeric string of length 10. By default, the value of `keyLength` prop used to generate the key is 6.

When you navigate back and forth between the /dashboard and /user paths by using the navigation links, you'll notice that a new key is generated for every navigation. This is because will you navigate using the navigation links, history.push is called and a new key is generated, and the key is unique for each entry in the history stack. Thus, when you navigate by clicking the browser's back button, history.pop is called, and you'll notice that the key generated for the location is shown and a new key is not generated.

getUserConfirmation prop

The getUserConfirmation prop accepts a function as its value, and it's executed when the user-initiated navigation is blocked using the <Prompt> component. The <Prompt> component shows a confirmation dialog box using the window.confirm method, and navigates the user to the selected path only if the user clicks the **OK** button. However, when the <BrowserRouter> component specifies the getUserConfirmation prop, the function provided as a value to this prop will be executed. This provides an opportunity to display a custom dialog box.

Let's take a look at the following configuration:

```
<BrowserRouter getUserConfirmation={this.userConfirmationFunc}>
    <div className="container">
        <nav>
            <Link to="/dashboard">Dashboard</Link>
            <Link to="/user">User</Link>
        </nav>
        <Route
            path="/dashboard"
            render={({ location }) =>
                <div> In Dashboard, Location Key: {location.key} </div>
            }
        />
        <Route
            path="/user"
            render={({ location }) =>
                <div> In User, Location Key: {location.key}
                    <Prompt message="This is shown in a confirmation
                        window" />
                </div>
            }
        />
    </div>
</BrowserRouter>
```

Suppose the current URL path is /user and you try to navigate to a different route, such as /dashboard, by clicking the navigation link provided in the nav menu. The <Prompt> message will be shown if the getUserConfirmation prop is not specified. In this case, the function userConfirmationFunc, which is defined in the component's class, is executed.

You can call window.confirm to display a confirmation dialog box asking the user about the navigation:

```
userConfirmationFunc = (message, callback) => {
    const status = window.confirm(message);
    callback(status);
}
```

The function accepts two parameters—message and callback. The message parameter specifies the message that needs to be displayed, and the message prop included in the <Prompt> component provides this value. The function is expected to execute the callback function provided as the second parameter.

Here, a callback function is provided as the second parameter by the <BrowserRouter>. The window.confirm function is called with the provided message, and the user is presented with two buttons—**OK** and **CANCEL**; on clicking **OK**, status is set to true, and, on clicking **CANCEL**, status is set to false. The callback function provided as the second parameter is called with this status value; it is a true value that allows the user to navigate to the selected route.

This the default behavior; a native-browser-confirmation dialog box is shown before allowing the user to navigate to the selected page. However, this behavior can be changed in the userConfirmationFunc mentioned previously; you can show a custom dialog box instead of displaying the browser's native-confirmation dialog box.

Showing a custom dialog box using the getUserConfirmation prop

For the purpose of this example, let's add material-UI, which includes a custom dialog box component:

```
npm install --save @material-ui/core
```

Let's create a custom dialog box that wraps the Dialog component in @material-ui/core:

```
import {
    Button,
    Dialog,
    DialogActions,
    DialogContent,
    DialogTitle
} from '@material-ui/core';

export class ConfirmationDialog extends Component {
    render() {
        const { message, handleClose, isOpen } = this.props;
        return (
            <Dialog open={isOpen}>
                <DialogTitle>Custom Prompt</DialogTitle>
                <DialogContent>{message}</DialogContent>
                <DialogActions>
                    <Button onClick={handleClose.bind(this, true)}>
                    OK
                    </Button>
                    <Button onClick={handleClose.bind(this, false)}>
                    CANCEL
                    </Button>
                </DialogActions>
            </Dialog>
        )
    }
}
```

This component accepts three props—message, handleClose, and isOpen. The message prop is the message that you want to show in the custom dialog box, and the handleClose prop is a function reference provided to the component that is invoked when the user clicks on the buttons **OK** or **CANCEL**, which allow or cancel the transition to the selected path, respectively.

Let's use this in our root component file (in App.js), and show the ConfirmationDialog when the user tries to navigate to a different route:

```
class App extends Component {
    state = {
        showConfirmationDialog: false,
        message: '',
        callback: null
    }
    ...
```

[83]

We will first set the `state` properties to their initial values in the React Component. The `state` properties mentioned previously change when the user tries to navigate to a different route:

```
...
userConfirmationFunc = (message, callback) => {
    this.setState({
        showConfirmationDialog: true,
        message: message,
        callback: callback
    });
}
```

The preceding `userConfirmationFunc` function sets the `state` properties such that it will display the custom confirmation dialog box (`ConfirmationDialog`) when the user tries to navigate away from the current route.

The following `handleClose` function, defined in the `App` component, will be provided to the `ConfirmationDialog` component that we created earlier:

```
...
handleClose(status) {
    this.state.callback(status);
    this.setState({
        showConfirmationDialog: false,
        message: '',
        callback: null
    })
}
```

This provides us with a way to hide the custom confirmation dialog box and to reset the component's `state` properties to their initial values.

The `this.state.callback(status)` statement will close the confirmation dialog box, and either navigate the user to the selected route (if the status is true) or cancel the navigation (if the status is false).

Here's the updated render method of the component class:

```
...
render() {
    return (
        <BrowserRouter
            getUserConfirmation={this.userConfirmationFunc}>
            ...
            <Route
                path="/user"
```

```
                render={({ location }) => {
                    return (
                      <div>
                        In User, Location Key: {location.key}
                        <Prompt message="This is shown in a
                          confirmation modal" />
                      </div>
                    );
                }}
            />
            <ConfirmationDialog
                isOpen={this.state.showConfirmationDialog}
                message={this.state.message}
                handleClose={this.handleClose.bind(this)}
            />
            ...
        </BrowserRouter>
      )
    }
}
```

In the preceding render method, the custom `ConfirmationDialog` box is included, and it's rendered only if the state property `showConrfirmationDialog` is set to `true`. The `userConfirmationFunc` sets the `state` properties and the custom dialog is shown as follows:

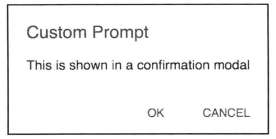

The `handleClose` function in the preceding code snippet is called by the `ConfirmDialog` box when the user clicks either of the buttons **OK** or **CANCEL**. The **OK** button will send the value `true`, whereas the **CANCEL** button sends a `false` value to the `handleClose` function defined previously.

<HashRouter> component

The <HashRouter> component is part of the react-router-dom package, and, similar to <BrowserRouter>, it's also used in building applications for the browser environment. The primary difference between <BrowserRouter> and <HashRouter> is the URL that the component creates:

A <BrowserRouter> creates a URL as follows:

www.packtpub.com/react-router

Whereas the <HashRouter> adds a hash to the URL:

www.packtpub.com/#/react-router

The <BrowserRouter> component leverages the HTML5 History API to keep track of the router history, whereas the <HashRouter> component uses window.location.hash (the hash portion of the URL) to remember the changes in the browser's history stack. The <BrowserRouter> should be used in building applications that work on modern browsers that support the HTML5's History API, and the <HashRouter> should be used in applications that need to support legacy browsers.

The <HashRouter> uses the createHashHistory class to create the history object. This history object is then provided to the core <Router> component:

```
import { createHashHistory as createHistory } from "history";

class HashRouter extends React.Component {
    ...
    history = createHistory(this.props);
    ...
    render() {
        return <Router
                history={this.history}
                children={this.props.children}
            />;
    }
}
```

The `<HashRouter>` accepts the following props:

```
static propTypes = {
    basename: PropTypes.string,
    getUserConfirmation: PropTypes.func,
    hashType: PropTypes.oneOf(["hashbang", "noslash", "slash"]),
    children: PropTypes.node
};
```

Similar to `<BrowserRouter>`, the props `basename` and `getUserConfirmation` are used to specify the base URL path and function to confirm navigation to the selected URL respectively. However, the `<HashRouter>` does not support `location.key` and `location.state`, thus the prop `keyLength` is not supported. Also, the prop `forceRefresh` is not supported.

Let's take a look at the `hashType` prop.

hashType prop

The `hashType` prop is used to specify the encoding method to use for `window.location.hash`. The possible values are `slash`, `noslash`, and `hashbang`.

Let's take a look at how the URLs are formed when you include the `hashType` prop with one of these values:

```
<HashRouter hashType="slash">
    <App />
</HashRouter>
```

When you specify `slash` as the value to the `hashType` prop, a slash (/) is added after the hash (#). Thus, the URLs will be of the forms —#/, #/dashboard, #/user, and so on.

Please note, `slash` is the default value for the prop `hashType`, and it's not required to include the `hashType` prop when you want to add a slash after the #.

Similarly, when the value of the `hashType` prop is `noslash`, the URLs are of the forms —#, #dashboard, #user, and so on:

```
<HashRouter hashType="noslash">
```

[87]

When the value `hashbang` is assigned to the `hashType` prop, it creates URLs of the form—`#!/`, `#!/dashboard`, `#!/user`, and so on:

`<HashRouter hashType="hashbang">`

The `hashbang` was added so that the search engine bots can crawl and index single-page application. However, Google has deprecated this crawling strategy. Read about it here: `https://webmasters.googleblog.com/2015/10/deprecating-our-ajax-crawling-scheme.html`.

Summary

The `<Router>` component in the `react-router` package provides a low-level implementation of the router interface. Various routers in `react-router-dom` and `react-router-native` use this low-level `<Router>` interface to provide routing features for the given environment. The `history` prop in `<Router>` is used to specify the `history` object for the given environment. For example, the `<BrowserRouter>` component uses `history/createBrowserHistory` to create a `history` object in the browser environment. All the Router components accept only one child, and it's usually the application's root component.

The `BrowserRouter` component in `react-router-dom` makes use of the HTML5 history API to keep the application's URL in sync with the browser's history. It accepts props—basename, keyLength, forceRefresh, and getUserConfirmation. The `<HashRouter>`, on the other hand, adds a hash (#) to the browser's URL and uses `window.location.hash` to track history. It accepts props basename, getUserConfirmation, and hashType. The hashType prop is used to specify the encoding method to use for `window.location.hash`; possible values are `slash`, `noslash`, and `hashbang`.

In Chapter 6, *Using StaticRouter in a Server-Side Rendered React Application*, we will take a look at server-side rendering with the `<StaticRouter>` component.

6
Using StaticRouter in a Server-Side Rendered React Application

Server-Side Rendering (**SSR**) is a technique of rendering client-side only **single-page applications** (**SPAs**) on the server and sending the fully rendered page as a response to the user's request. In client-side SPAs, the JavaScript bundle is included as a script tag, and, initially, no content is rendered in the page. The bundle is first downloaded, and then the DOM nodes are populated by executing the code in the bundle. There are two downsides to this—on poor connections, it might take more time to download the bundle, and the crawlers that don't execute JavaScript will not be able to see any content, thus affecting the page's SEO.

SSR solves these problems by loading HTML, CSS, and JavaScript in response to the user's request; the content is rendered on the server and the final HTML is given to the crawler. A React application can be rendered on the server using Node.js and the components available in React-Router can be used to define routes in the application.

In this chapter, we will take a look at how React-Router components can be used in a server-side rendered React application:

- Performing SSR of a React application using Node.js and Express.js
- Adding `<StaticRouter>` component and creating routes
- Understanding the `<StaticRouter>` props
- Creating Isomorphic React applications by rendering the first page on the server and then allowing the client-side code to take over the rendering of subsequent pages

Performing SSR of a React application using Node.js and Express.js

In this example, we will use Node.js and Express.js to create a server-side application that will render the React application on the server. Node.js is a cross-platform JavaScript runtime environment for servers and applications. It is built on Google's V8 JavaScript engine, and it uses an event-driven, non-blocking I/O model, which makes it efficient and lightweight. Express.js is one of the most popular routing and middleware web-framework modules used in the Node.js environment. It allows you to create middleware that helps with handling HTTP requests from clients.

Installing dependencies

Let's first create a server-side application using the `npm init` command:

```
npm init -y
```

This will create a file, `package.json`, with default values for various fields. The next step is to add dependencies:

```
npm install --save react react-dom react-router react-router-dom express
```

The preceding command will add all the necessary libraries to the `dependencies` list in the package.json file. Please note that we are not creating a React application using the `create-react-app` CLI; instead, we will add the required dependencies and write the configuration files for building the application.

To build the application, the following dev dependencies are added to the `devDependencies` list:

```
npm install --save-dev webpack webpack-cli nodemon-webpack-plugin webpack-node-externals babel-core babel-loader babel-preset-env babel-preset-react
```

The preceding command will add the libraries required to build the application for the `devDependencies` list in the `package.json` file.

The next step is to write a build configuration, so that the server-side application can be built.

Webpack build configuration

This is from Webpack's documentation:

> At its core, **WebPack** is a static module bundler for modern JavaScript applications. When webpack processes your application, it internally builds a dependency graph which maps every module your project needs and generates one or more bundles.

Webpack has become the de facto standard for creating bundles for JavaScript applications. The `create-react-app` CLI includes scripts that internally use `webpack` to create bundles for development and production environments.

Create a file called `webpack-server.config.babel.js`, and include the following configuration:

```js
import path from 'path';
import webpack from 'webpack';
import nodemonPlugin from 'nodemon-webpack-plugin';
import nodeExternals from 'webpack-node-externals';

export default {
    entry: './src/server/index.js',
    target: 'node',
    externals: [nodeExternals()],
    output: {
        path: path.resolve(__dirname, 'dist'),
        filename: 'server.js',
        publicPath: '/'
    },
    module: {
        rules: [
            {
                test: /\.js$/,
                use: 'babel-loader'
            }
        ]
    },
    plugins: [
        new webpack.DefinePlugin({
            __isBrowser__: false
        }),
        new nodemonPlugin()
    ]
}
```

From the preceding configuration, the file `index.js` (at the `./src/server` path) is mentioned as the entry point, and the generated output file `server.js` is copied to the `dist` directory. The `webpack` plugin `babel-loader` is used to transpile JavaScript files in the application using `Babel` and `Webpack`. The `nodemon-webpack-plugin` is used to run the `nodemon` utility, which will monitor the changes in the JavaScript files in the application, and reload and build the application when `webpack` is running in watch mode.

The next step is to create a `.babelrc` file, which will list the presets required to build the application:

```
{
  "presets": ["env","react"]
}
```

The `babel-preset-env` and `babel-preset-react` plugins are used to transpile ES6 and React code down to ES5. As the last step, add a script command in the `package.json` file to start the application using the configuration mentioned in the `webpack-server.config.babel.js` file:

```
"scripts": {
    "start": "webpack --config webpack-server.config.babel.js --watch --mode development"
}
```

The command `npm start` will build the application, and will listen to the changes in the JavaScript files in the application and rebuild it when a change is detected.

Server-Side application

As mentioned in the `webpack` configuration, the entry point to the application is at `/src/server/index.js`. Let's create the `index.js` file at this path, and include the following code, which starts the server application at a given port:

```
import express from 'express';

const PORT = process.env.PORT || 3001;

const app = express();

app.get('*', (req, res) => {
    res.send(`
        <!DOCTYPE HTML>
        <html>
            <head>
```

```
                <title>React SSR example</title>
            </head>
            <body>
                <main id='app'>Rendered on the server side</main>
            </body>
        </html>
    `);
});

app.listen(PORT, () => {
    console.log(`SSR React Router app running at ${PORT}`);
});
```

When you run the `npm start` command and access the application at the URL `http://localhost:3001`, the preceding HTML content is rendered. This ensures that the `webpack` configuration builds the application and runs the preceding server-side code at port `3001`, with `nodemon` monitoring the changes in the file.

Rendering a React application using ReactDOMServer.renderToString

To render a React application on the server-side, let's first create a React component file —`shared/App.js`:

```
import React, { Component } from 'react';

export class App extends Component {
    render() {
        return (
            <div>Inside React App (rendered with SSR)</div>
        );
    }
}
```

Then, render the preceding component in the `server/index.js` file:

```
import express from 'express';
import React from 'react';
import ReactDOMServer from 'react-dom/server';
import { App } from '../shared/App';

app.get('*', (req, res) => {
```

Using StaticRouter in a Server-Side Rendered React Application

```
        const reactMarkup = ReactDOMServer.renderToString(<App />);
        res.send(`
            <!DOCTYPE HTML>
            <html>
            ...
                <main id='app'>${reactMarkup}</main>
            ...
            </html>
        `);
    });
```

The `ReactDOMServer` class includes various methods for rendering React components in a server-side Node.js application. The `renderToString` method in `ReactDOMServer` class renders the React component on the server-side and returns the generated markup. This generated markup string can then be included in the response being sent to the user.

When you visit the page at `http://localhost:3001`, you will notice that the message **Inside React App (rendered with SSR)** is displayed.

To confirm that the content is indeed rendered on the server-side, you can right click on the page and select the **View page source** option from the context menu. The page source is shown in a new tab, and it includes the following content:

```
<main id='app'>
    <div data-reactroot="">
        Inside React App (rendered with SSR)
    </div>
</main>
```

The preceding content is helpful when the crawler visits the application. By rendering the React component on the server-side, the markup is populated and included as the response from the server. This content is then indexed by the search engine's crawler, helping with the application's SEO aspects.

Adding <StaticRouter> and creating routes

The `<StaticRouter>` component is part of the `react-router-dom` package (uses `<StaticRouter>` definition in `react-router`), and it's used in rendering React-Router components on the server-side. The `<StaticRouter>` component is similar to the other Router components, as it accepts only one child component—the React application's root component (`<App />`). This component should be used in a stateless application, where the user is not clicking around to navigate to different sections of the page.

Let's include the `<StaticRouter>` component by wrapping the application's root component:

```
import { StaticRouter } from 'react-router-dom';

app.get('*', (req, res) => {
    const context = {};
    const reactMarkup = ReactDOMServer.renderToString(
        <StaticRouter context={context} location={req.url}>
            <App />
        </StaticRouter>
    );

    res.send(`
        ...
        <main id='app'>${reactMarkup}</main>
        ...
    `);
});
```

Notice that the `<StaticRouter>` component accepts two props—`context` and `location`. The `context` object is an empty object and is populated with properties when one of the `<Route>` components inside `<App />` is rendered as a result of the browser's location match.

The `location` object is usually the requested URL, and this information is available to the middleware function. The request object (`req`) contains the `url` property specifying the requested URL.

Let's include a couple of `<Route>` components in `App.js`:

```
export class App extends Component {
    render() {
        return (
            <div>
                Inside React App (rendered with SSR)
                <Route
                    exact
                    path='/'
                    render={() => <div>Inside Route at path '/'</div>}
                />
                <Route
                    path='/home'
                    render={() =>
                        <div>Inside Home Route at path '/home'</div>
                    }
```

[95]

```
            />
        </div>
    );
  }
}
```

The `<Route>` components match the requested URL specified in the `<StaticRouter>` component's `location` property and render.

Server-Side redirect using the <Redirect> and staticContext

From the previous example, let's redirect the user from the / path to the /home path using the `<Redirect>` component:

```
<Route
    path="/"
    render={() => <Redirect to="/home" />}
    exact
/>
```

When you try accessing the URL `http://localhost:3001/`, you will notice that the redirection does not take place and the browser's URL is not updated. The preceding redirect would have sufficed in the client-side environment. However, in the server-side environment, the server is responsible for handling the redirect. In this case, the `context` object mentioned in the `<StaticRouter>` component is populated with necessary details:

```
{
    "action": "REPLACE",
    "location": {
        "pathname": "/home",
        "search": "",
        "hash": "",
        "state": undefined
    },
    "url": "/home"
}
```

The `context` object contains the result of the component render. It's usually an empty object when the component renders just the content. However, it's populated with the preceding details when the rendered component redirects to a different path. Notice that the `url` property specifies the path to which the user should be redirected—to the `'/home'` path.

A check can be added to see if the `url` property exists in the `context` object, and then the user can be redirected by using the `redirect` method on the `response` object:

```
...
const reactMarkup = ReactDOMServer.renderToString(
    <StaticRouter context={context} location={req.url}>
        <App />
    </StaticRouter>
);

if (context.url) {
    res.redirect(301, 'http://' + req.headers.host + context.url);
} else {
    res.send(`
        <!DOCTYPE HTML>
        <html>
            ...
        </html>
    `);
}
```

The `redirect` method in the `response` object is used to perform the server-side redirection, and mentions the status code and the URL to redirect to.

It's also possible to populate the `context` object with more properties by using the `staticContext` prop in the rendered component:

```
<Route
    path="/"
    exact
    render={({ staticContext, }) => {
        if (staticContext) {
            staticContext.status = 301;
        }
        return (
            <Redirect to="/home" />
        )
    }}
/>
```

Here, the `staticContext` prop is available in the rendered component, and the `status` property is added to it before redirecting the user using the `<Redirect>` component. The `status` property is then available in the `context` object:

```
res.redirect(context.status, 'http://' + req.headers.host + context.url);
```

Here, the `status` property in the `context` object is used to set the HTTP status when the user is redirected using the `redirect` method.

Request URL matching with matchPath

When rendering the React application on the server-side, it is also helpful to know whether the requested URL matches any of the existing routes in the application. Only if the route is available should the corresponding component be rendered on the server-side. However, if the route is not available, the user should be presented with a Page Not Found page (404). The `matchPath` function in the `react-router` package allows you match the requested URL against an object containing route-matching properties such as `path`, `exact`, `strict`, and `sensitive`:

```
import { matchPath } from 'react-router'

app.use('*', (req, res) => {
    const isRouteAvailable = matchPath(req.url, {
        path: '/dashboard/',
        strict: true
    });
    ...

});
```

The `matchPath` function is similar to how the library matches `<Route>` components against the requested URL path. The first parameter passed to the `matchPath` function is the requested URL, and the second parameter is the object against which the requested URL should be matched. When the route matches, the `matchPath` function returns an object detailing how the requested URL matched the object.

For example, if the requested URL is `/dashboard/`, the `matchPath` function returns the following object:

```
{
    path: '/dashboard/',
    url: '/dashboard/',
    isExact: true,
    params: {}
}
```

Here, the `path` property mentions the path pattern used to match the requested URL, the `url` property mentions the matched portion of the URL, the `isExact` Boolean property is set to `true` if the requested URL and path matched exactly, and the `params` property lists the params that matched the provided pathname. Consider the following example, which mentions parameters in the path:

```
const matchedObject = matchPath(req.url, '/github/:githubID');
```

Here, instead of specifying an object as a second parameter, a path string is specified. This short notation is useful if you want to match the path against the requested URL, and use the default values for the `exact`, `strict`, and `sensitive` properties. The matched object will return the following:

```
{
    path: '/github/:githubID',
    url: '/github/sagar.ganatra',
    isExact: true,
    params: { githubID: 'sagar.ganatra' }
}
```

Notice that the `params` property is now populated with the list of params mentioned in the `path`, with the values provided in the requested URL.

On the server-side, before initializing the `<StaticRouter>` and rendering the React application, a check can be performed to see if the requested URL matches any of the routes defined in a collection of objects. For example, consider a collection of route objects.

In `shared/routes.js` we have the following:

```
export const ROUTES = [
    {
        path: '/',
        exact: true
    },
    {
        path: '/dashboard/',
        strict: true
    },
    {
        path: '/github/:githubId'
    }
];
```

Using StaticRouter in a Server-Side Rendered React Application

The preceding array contains route objects that can then be used in `matchPath` to check if the requested URL matches any of the routes in the preceding list:

```
app.get('*', (req, res) => {
    const isRouteAvailable = ROUTES.find(route => {
        return matchPath(req.url, route);
    })
    ...
});
```

If the requested URL is found, then `isRouteAvailalbe` will be the matched object in the `ROUTES` list, else it's set to `undefined` when none of the route objects match the requested URL. In the latter case, a Page Not Found markup can be sent to the user:

```
if (!isRouteAvailable) {
    res.status(404);
    res.send(`
        <!DOCTYPE HTML>
        <html>
            <head><title>React SSR example</title></head>
            <body>
                <main id='app'>
                    Requested page '${req.url}' not found
                </main>
            </body>
        </html>`);
    res.end();
}
```

When the user requests a path, say `/user`, none of the objects mentioned in the `ROUTES` would match, and the preceding response is sent, mentioning the `404` HTTP status, with the response body mentioning that the requested path `/user` was not found.

StaticRouter context prop

The `<StaticRouter>` component accepts props `basename`, `location`, and `context`. Similar to other Router implementations, the `basename` prop in `<StaticRouter>` is used to specify the `baseURL` location and the `location`, prop is used to specify the location properties—`pathname`, `hash`, `search`, and `state`.

The `context` prop is used only in the `<StaticRouter>` implementation, and it contains the result of the component render. As mentioned previously, the `context` object can be populated with an HTTP status code and with other arbitrary properties as well.

At the time of initialization, the context object can contain properties that can then be consumed by the rendered component:

```
const context = {
    message: 'From StaticRouter\'s context object'
}
const reactMarkup = ReactDOMServer.renderToString(
    <StaticRouter context={context} location={req.url} >
        <App />
    </StaticRouter>
);
```

Here, the context object contains a message property, and when the <Route> component that matches the requested URL is found, the staticContext object containing this property is available to the rendered component:

```
<Route
    path='/home'
    render={({ staticContext }) => {
        return (
            <div>
                Inside Home Route, Message - {staticContext.message}
            </div>
        );
    }}
/>
```

When you try to access the /home path, the preceding <Route> matches and the value mentioned in the staticContext message property is rendered.

The staticContext prop is available only in the server-side environment, and thus, when you try to refer the staticContext object in an isomorphic application (discussed in the next section), an error stating that you're trying to access the property message of undefined is thrown. A check can be added to see if the staticContext is available or if the value of the __isBrowser__ property defined in the webpack configuration can be checked:

```
<Route
    path='/home'
    render={({ staticContext }) => {
        if (!__isBrowser__) {
            return (
                <div>
                    Inside Home Route, Message - {staticContext.message}
                </div>
```

```
                );
            }
            return (
                <div>Inside Home Route, Message</div>
            );
        }}
    />
```

In the preceding example, if the page is rendered on the server-side, then the `__isBrowser__` property will be `false` and the message specified in the `staticContext` object will be rendered.

Creating Isomorphic React applications

An application where the code can run on server-and client-side environments with little or no change is referred to as an Isomorphic application. In an Isomorphic application, the first request made by the user's web browser is processed by the server, and any subsequent request is processed by the client. By processing and rendering the first request on the server-side, and sending HTML, CSS, and JavaScript code provides a better user experience, and also helps search engine crawlers to index the page. All subsequent requests can then be processed by the client-side code, which is sent as part of the first response from the server.

Here's the updated request-response flow:

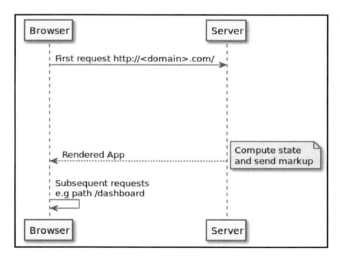

To render the application on the client-side, either of the `<BrowserRouter>` or `<HashRouter>` components can be used. For the purpose of this example, we will use the `<BrowserRouter>` component.

The application structure after adding a directory for the client-side code is as follows:

```
/server-side-app
|--/src
|----/client
|------index.js
|----/server
|------index.js
|----/shared
|------App.js
```

Here, the `shared` directory will contain code that can be used by both the server-and the client-side code. The client-side specific code that uses the `<BrowserRouter>` component resides in the `index.js` file in the `client` directory:

```
import React from "react";
import ReactDOM from "react-dom";
import { BrowserRouter } from "react-router-dom";
import { App } from "../shared/App";

// using hydrate instead of render in SSR app
ReactDOM.hydrate(
    <BrowserRouter>
        <App />
    </BrowserRouter>,
    document.getElementById("app")
);
```

Here, the `hydrate` method in the `ReactDOM` class is used instead of calling the `render` method to render the application. The `hydrate` method is specifically designed to handle cases where the initial render happens on the server-side (using `ReactDOMServer`), and all the subsequent route-change requests to update specific sections of the page are handled by the client-side code. The `hydrate` method is used to attach event listeners to the markup rendered on the server-side.

The next step is to build the application, so that the client-side bundle is generated at the build time and included in the first response from the server.

Webpack configuration

The existing webpack configuration builds the server-side application and runs the `nodemon` utility to monitor the changes. To generate a client-side bundle, we need to include another webpack configuration file—`webpack-client.config.babel.js`:

```
import path from 'path';
import webpack from 'webpack';

export default {
    entry: './src/client/index.js',
    output: {
        path: path.resolve(__dirname, './dist/public'),
        filename: 'bundle.js',
        publicPath: '/'
    },
    module: {
        rules: [
            {
                test: /\.js$/,
                use: 'babel-loader'
            }
        ]
    },
    plugins: [
        new webpack.DefinePlugin({
            __isBrowser__: "true"
        })
    ]
}
```

The preceding configuration resolves the dependencies in the `/src/client/index.js` file and creates a bundle at `/dist/public/bundle.js`. This bundle contains all the client-side code required to run the application; not only the code in the `index.js` file but also the components declared in the `shared` directory.

The current `npm start` script also needs to be modified so that the client-side application code builds along with the server-side code. Let's create a file that exports both the server and client webpack configurations—`webpack.config.babel.js`:

```
import clientConfig from './webpack-client.config.babel';
import serverConfig from './webpack-server.config.babel';

export default [clientConfig, serverConfig];
```

Finally, the `npm start` script is updated to refer to the preceding configuration file:

```
"start": "webpack --config webpack.config.babel.js --mode development --watch"
```

The preceding script will generate `server.js`, which contains the server-side code, and `bundle.js`, which contains the client-side code.

Server-Side configuration

The last step is to update the server-side code to include the client-side bundle (`bundle.js`) as part of the first response. The server-side code can include a `<script>` tag which specifies the `bundle.js` file in the source (`src`) attribute:

```
res.send(`
    <!DOCTYPE HTML>
    <html>
        <head>
            <title>React SSR example</title>
            <script src='/bundle.js' defer></script>
            ...
        </html>
`);
```

Also, for our express server to serve a JavaScript file, we include the middleware function for serving static content:

```
app.use(express.static('dist/public'))
```

The preceding code allows static files such as JavaScript files, CSS files, and Images, to be served from the `dist/public` directory. The preceding statement should be included before `app.get()` is used.

When you access the application at the `/home` path, the first response is from the server, and, in addition to rendering the `<Route>` that matched the `/home` path, the client-side bundle—`bundle.js`—is also included in the response. The `bundle.js` file is downloaded by the browser, and any change in the route path is then handled by the client-side code.

Summary

In this chapter, we looked at how a React application can be rendered on the server-side (with Node.js and Express.js) using the `ReactDOMserver.renderToString` method. The `<StaticRouter>` component in React-Router can be used to wrap the application's root component, thus enabling you to add `<Route>` components that match the requested URL path on the server-side. The `<StaticRouter>` component accepts props `context` and `location`. The `staticContext` prop (available only on the server-side) in the rendered component contains the data provided by the `<StaticRouter>` in the `context` prop. It can also be used to add properties when you want to redirect the user using the `<Redirect>` component.

The `matchPath` function is used to determine whether the requested URL matches the provided object of the shape `{path, exact, strict, sensitive}`. It's similar to how the library matches the requested URL with the available `<Route>` components in the page. The `matchPath` function gives us the ability to determine if the requested URL matches any of the routes object in the collection; this provides us with an opportunity to send a 404: Page not found response up front.

It's also possible to create an isomorphic React application that renders the first request on the server-side and the subsequent requests on the client side. This is accomplished by including the client-side bundle file when sending the first response from the server. The client-side code takes over after the first request, which enables you to update specific sections of the page that match the requested route.

In `Chapter 7`, *Using NativeRouter in a React Native Application*, we will take a look at how the `NativeRouter` component can be used to define routes in a native mobile application created with React-Native.

7
Using NativeRouter in a React Native Application

The React Router library provides the `react-router-native` package, which includes the implementation of the `NativeRouter` component for use in React Native applications. The React Native framework allows you to build native mobile applications for iOS and Android using JavaScript and React.

From React Native's Documentation (`https://facebook.github.io/react-native/`):

> "With React Native, you don't build a **mobile web app**, an **HTML5 app**, or a **hybrid app**. You build a real mobile app that's indistinguishable from an app built using Objective-C or Java. React Native uses the same fundamental UI building blocks as regular iOS and Android apps. You just put those building blocks together using JavaScript and React."

In this chapter, the following topics are discussed:

- Using NativeRouter in a React Native application
- The NativeRouter component and its props
- Using the `<BackButton>` component to interact with a devices' back button
- Creating Deeplinks using the `<DeepLinking>` component

Using NativeRouter in a React Native application

Similar to the `create-react-app` CLI, the `create-react-native-app` CLI is used to create an application that includes build scripts that can be used to build an application for both development and production environments. It also includes `packager`, which allows you to test your application on iOS and Android emulators and also on real devices.

Creating a new project with the create-react-native-app CLI

Let's get started by first installing the CLI:

```
npm install -g create-react-native-app
```

The preceding command installs the CLI in the global `node_modules` directory. The next step is to create a React Native project using the CLI:

```
create-react-native-app react-native-test-app
```

The `react-native-test-app` directory is created and all the required scripts are downloaded in the `node_modules` directory.

Now, when you run the `npm start` script, the build script starts `packager` and it generates a QR code and a URL for you to access the application on a real device (iOS or Android) or on the emulator. Also, you could launch the iOS or Android emulator if you have Xcode or Android Studio installed. Here's an example:

```
Your app is now running at URL: exp://192.168.1.100:19000
View your app with live reloading:
Android device:
-> Point the Expo app to the QR code above.
(You'll find the QR scanner on the Projects tab of the app.)
iOS device:
-> Press s to email/text the app URL to your phone.
Emulator:
-> Press a (Android) or i (iOS) to start an emulator.
Your phone will need to be on the same local network as this computer.
For links to install the Expo app, please visit https://expo.io.
Logs from serving your app will appear here. Press Ctrl+C at any time to stop.
› Press a to open Android device or emulator, or i to open iOS emulator.
```

```
› Press s to send the app URL to your phone number or email address
› Press q to display QR code.
› Press r to restart packager, or R to restart packager and clear cache.
› Press d to toggle development mode. (current mode: development)
```

For the purpose of this example, we will use the Xcode emulator; here's a screenshot of the application when you request the application to be viewed on the iOS emulator:

React Native provides several components that allow you to build views for the native platform. Let's take a look at the code and understand some of the components used to build the preceding view.

In `App.js`, the following code is included:

```
export default class App extends React.Component {
    render() {
        return (
            <View style={styles.container}>
                <Text>Open up App.js to start working on your app!</Text>
                <Text>Changes you make will automatically reload.</Text>
                <Text>Shake your phone to open the developer menu.</Text>
            </View>
        );
    }
}
```

Here, React Native's `<View>` component is used to create a container in a similar way to how you would create a container using `<div>` or `<section>` in a React application. In React Native, instead of using HTML elements, such as `<div>` and `<span>`, React Native's components, such as `<View>` and `<Text>`, are used.

Adding the <NativeRouter> component

Let's now add the `react-router-native` package to the application that we just created:

```
npm install --save react-router-native
```

The `NativeRouter` component is used in React Native applications to provide routing and navigation support. It enables components such as `<Route>` and `<Link>` to be used in the native application.

Let's first create a side menu that includes a couple of `<Link>` components:

```
import { Link } from 'react-router-native';

export class Menu extends Component {
    render() {
        return (
            <ScrollView scrollsToTop={false} style={styles.menu}>
                <View>
                    <Link to="/">
                        <Text>Home</Text>
                    </Link>
```

```
                <Link to="/dashboard">
                    <Text>Dashboard</Text>
                </Link>
            </View>
        </ScrollView>
    )
}
}
```

The `<ScrollView>` component is used as a container to host our menu items (the `<Link>` components). As the name suggests, the `<ScrollView>` component is used to create a scrollable container. The next step is to add `<Route>` components to the application:

```
export class ContentView extends Component {
    render() {
        return (
            <View style={styles.container}>
                <Route
                    path="/"
                    exact
                    component={HomeComponent}
                />
                <Route
                    path="/dashboard"
                    component={DashboardComponent}
                />
            </View>
        )
    }
}
```

The `ContentView` component wraps the `<Route>` components inside a `<View>` component, thus defining two application routes with path `/` and `/dashboard`.

As the last step, we will now use the `<SideMenu>` component from `react-native-side-menu` to create a drawer menu. This menu is then wrapped inside the `<NativeRouter>` component in App.js:

```
export default class App extends Component {
    render() {
        const menu = <Menu />;
        return (
            <NativeRouter>
                <View style={styles.container}>
                    <SideMenu menu={menu}>
                        <ContentView />
                    </SideMenu>
```

Using NativeRouter in a React Native Application

```
                </View>
            </NativeRouter>
        );
    }
}
```

Similar to other Router implementations, the `NativeRouter` component wraps the application root component and enables the `<Route>` and `<Link>` components to update `history` as the user navigates through the application.

After rebuilding the application on the emulator:

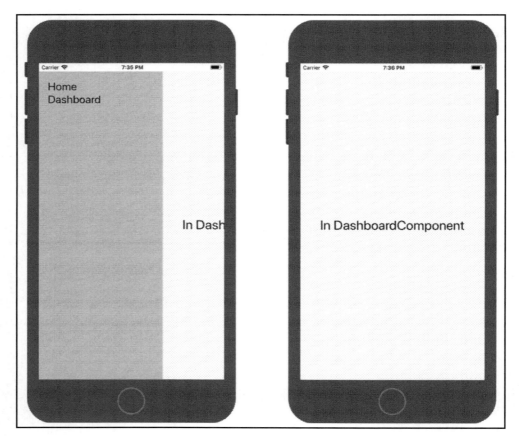

When you select either of the links, ContentView is updated with the component rendered as a result of a <Route> match.

The preceding functionality is similar to how BrowserRouter enables you to navigate through various routes defined in the application. Similar to the <Route> and <Link> components, other components such as <Switch>, <Redirect>, and <NavLink> behave the same in a React Native application. However, when you try to block the navigation using the <Prompt> component, React Native's Alert component should be used to display a confirmation message.

From NativeRouter's implementation:

```
import { Alert } from "react-native";

NativeRouter.defaultProps = {
    getUserConfirmation: (message, callback) => {
        Alert.alert("Confirm", message, [
            { text: "Cancel", onPress: () => callback(false) },
            { text: "OK", onPress: () => callback(true) }
        ]);
    }
};
```

NativeRouter provides a default implementation of the getUserConfirmation function, which makes use of the Alert component defined in the react-native package to display a confirmation message to the user:

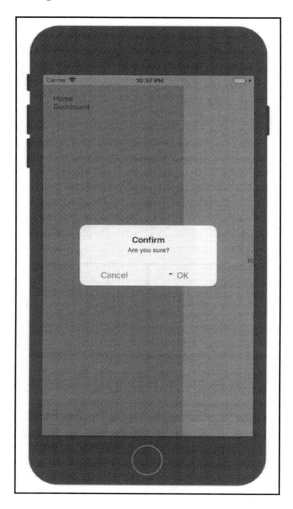

This default behavior can be overridden by including the getUserConfirmation prop:

```
<NativeRouter getUserConfirmation={customGetUserConfirmation}>
...
</NativeRouter>
```

The <NativeRouter> component

The NativeRouter component uses the MemoryRouter component defined in the react-router package to provide routing support in a React Native application. MemoryRouter is used when you want to maintain the browsing history in memory without updating the URL in the address bar. It's particularly useful in non-browser environments where an address bar is not available. The MemoryRouter component creates a history object using the createMemoryHistory class available in the history package. This history object is then provided to the low-level <Router> interface.

In NativeRotuer.js:

```
import MemoryRouter from "react-router/MemoryRouter";
const NativeRouter = props => <MemoryRouter {...props} />;
```

Then the MemoryRouter component creates a history object using createMemoryHistory, in MemoryRouter.js:

```
import { createMemoryHistory as createHistory } from "history";
class MemoryRouter extends React.Component {
    history = createHistory(this.props);
    ...
    render() {
        return <Router
                history={this.history}
                children={this.props.children}
            />;
    }
}
```

The NativeRouter component accepts props: initialEntries, initialIndex, getUserConfirmation, keyLength, and children. As mentioned previously, a default implementation for getUserConfirmation is included in the NativeRouter class and both keyLength and children props behave similarly to other Router components, as mentioned in previous chapters.

Let's take a look at initialEntries and initialIndex props.

The initialEntries prop

The `initialEntries` prop is used to populate the history stack with a list of locations:

```
export default class App extends Component {
    render() {
        const initialEntries = ['/', '/dashboard'];
        return (
            <NativeRouter initialEntries={initialEntries}>
            ...
            </NativeRouter>
        );
    }
}
```

At the time of initializing `NativeRouter`, you could populate the history by providing an array of location paths. A location path could be a string or even an object of shape `{ pathname, search, hash, state }`:

```
const initialEntries = [
    '/',
    {
        pathname: '/dashboard',
        search: '',
        hash: 'test',
        state: { from: '/'}
    }
];
```

The initialIndex prop

The `initialIndex` prop is used to specify the index value of the location in the `initialEntries` array to render when the application loads. For example, if the `initialEntries` array has two locations listed, then an `initialIndex` value of 1 loads the second entry; that is, a `<Route>` instance matching the pathname mentioned as the second entry in `initialEntries` array is rendered:

```
export default class App extends Component {
    render() {
        const initialEntries = ['/', '/dashboard'];
        const initialIndex = 1;

        return (
            <NativeRouter
                initialEntries={initialEntries}
```

```
                initialIndex={initialIndex}>
                ...
            </NativeRouter>
        )
    }
}
```

In this example, the `initialIndex` value is set to `1` and thus the `<Route>` matching the location path `/dashboard` is rendered when the application loads.

The <BackButton> component

By default, when you press the back button on an Android device, the application exits instead of navigating the user to the previous state in the history. The React Native library includes a `BackHandler` class, which lets you customize the behavior of the devices' hardware back button. The `<BackButton>` component in React Router uses the `BackHandler` class to customize the behavior of the back button on an Android device:

```
import { NativeRouter, BackButton } from 'react-router-native';

export default class App extends Component {
    render() {
        return (
            <NativeRouter>
                <View style={styles.container}>
                    <BackButton />
                    <SideMenu menu={menu}>
                        <ContentView />
                    </SideMenu>
                </View>
            </NativeRouter>
        )
    }
}
```

The `<BackButton>` component can be included anywhere in the application. In the preceding example, the component is included in the root component and it does not include any child components. Please note that the `<BackButton>` component does not render anything on the viewport; rather, it facilitates the interaction with the devices' back button.

[117]

Here's the workflow:

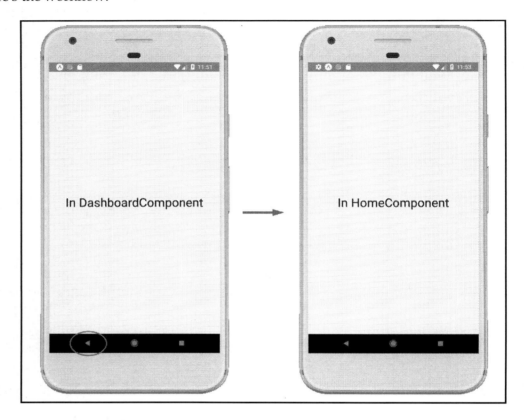

Whilst on the Dashboard screen (at path `/dashboard`), when you click the devices' back button, the user is navigated to the home page (at path `/`).

Creating Deeplinks with <DeepLinking>

In a web application, the HTTP URL refers to a location that can be accessed by entering the same in the address bar of the browser. In Single Page Applications, this location refers to a specific route that the user can navigate to. In the context of a mobile application, `DeepLink` refers to a specific page or content that you would want to view. For example, when you click on a link on a mobile device, instead of opening a new tab in the browser window, an application is launched and the requested page is shown.

Unlike web applications, which use HTTP to refer to a specific location, applications on a mobile device need to declare a URI scheme for the application. For example, the Twitter application uses the URI scheme `twitter://` and thus you could view their Twitter profile by referring to the URI `twitter://profile`. Deeplinks are very helpful when the user clicks on links in an email or accesses push notification messages, which navigate the user to the application to show the requested content.

React Native provides interfaces that allow you to create Deeplinks for devices on both iOS and Android platforms. In this section, we will take a look at how to create Deeplinks to an application's content on an Android device and thus we require Android Studio to be installed. Android Studio allows us to create virtual devices (AVD) that can then be used to test Deeplinks.

A step-by-step guide to installing the necessary components on iOS and Android is detailed in the React Native documentation: https://facebook.github.io/react-native/docs/getting-started.html.

After installing Android Studio and creating an AVD, the application needs to be configured with a URI scheme. To add the URI scheme, some of the native files need to be updated, and to get access to these native files, you need to eject from the current setup.

Ejecting from the create-react-native-app

The `create-react-native-app` CLI is a very good option for scaffolding a React Native application and for testing the application on an emulator. However, to test `DeepLinking` we would need to include entries in the manifest file and thus it's required that we eject from the configuration using the following command:

```
npm run eject
```

The previous command will generate configuration files for iOS and Android platforms. This bare-minimum configuration allows you to generate a `.ipa` file for an iOS device and a `.apk` file for an Android device. In this section, we will see how we can generate the `.apk` file, which will then be deployed to an AVD.

After ejecting, you will see various directories and files generated for both iOS and Android:

```
|--/android
|----/.gradle
|----/app
|----/build
|----/gradle
|----/keystores
|--/ios
|----/chapter7DeepLink
|----/chapter7DeepLink-tvOS
|----/chapter7DeepLink-tvOSTests
|----/chapter7DeepLink.Xcodeproj
|----/chapter7DeepLinkTests
```

The next step is to build and run the application on the Android device:

npm run android

The previous command will run the build script and generate the `.apk` file, which gets deployed on an AVD. Please ensure that you have the virtual device running before executing the previous command.

To configure the URI scheme on an Android device, the `AndroidManifest.xml` manifest file located at the `/android/app/src/main` path needs to be updated. In the next section, we will see the configuration that needs to be added to the manifest file.

Adding <intent-filter> to the manifest file

The `AndroidManifest.xml` file contains meta information about the application, and it is used to declare various components present in the application. These components are activated using intent filters. An `<intent-filter>` instance in the manifest file is used to define the capabilities of the application and in defining a policy on how other applications would interact with the application.

When you eject from the configuration, the `AndroidManifest.xml` file is generated:

```
<manifest
    xmlns:android="http://schemas.android.com/apk/res/android"
    package="com.chapter7deeplink">
    <uses-permission android:name="android.permission.INTERNET" />
    <uses-permission
android:name="android.permission.SYSTEM_ALERT_WINDOW"/>
    <application
        android:name=".MainApplication"
        android:label="@string/app_name"
        android:icon="@mipmap/ic_launcher"
        android:allowBackup="false"
        android:theme="@style/AppTheme">
        <activity
            android:name=".MainActivity"
            android:label="@string/app_name"
android:configChanges="keyboard|keyboardHidden|orientation|screenSize"
            android:windowSoftInputMode="adjustResize">
            <intent-filter>
                <action android:name="android.intent.action.MAIN" />
                <category android:name="android.intent.category.LAUNCHER"
/>
            </intent-filter>
        </activity>
        <activity
          android:name="com.facebook.react.devsupport.DevSettingsActivity" />
    </application>
</manifest>
```

Here, `<intent-filter>` has the action and the category defined for the application as `android.intent.action.MAIN` and `android.intent.category.LAUNCHER`. The previous `intent-filter` enables the application to be seen on the user's device and when the user taps on the application, `MainActivity` (see the activity tag) in the application is triggered.

Similarly, `intent-filter` for defining a URI scheme for the application can be added to the manifest file:

```
<intent-filter android:label="filter_react_native">
    <action android:name="android.intent.action.VIEW" />
    <category android:name="android.intent.category.DEFAULT" />
    <category android:name="android.intent.category.BROWSABLE" />
    <data android:scheme="deeplink" android:host="app.chapter7.com" />
</intent-filter>
```

Using NativeRouter in a React Native Application

Here, the `<data>` tag is used to specify the URI scheme for the application. The `android:scheme` attribute in the `<data>` tag is used to specify the scheme name and the `android:host` attribute is used to specify the type of `hostname` to use for the application. Thus the `deeplink://app.chapter7.com` URI is used to access the home page in the application. A route with the `/dashboard` path can be accessed using this URI: `deeplink://app.chapter7.com/dashboard`.

The next step is to use React Router's `<DeepLinking>` component so that the application can react to the incoming request and navigate the user to the request route.

Including the <DeepLinking> component

The `<DeepLinking>` component in the `react-router-native` package uses React Native's `Linking` interface to listen to the changes in the URL. Whenever a change is detected, the user is navigated to the requested path by adding an entry in the history stack.

The `<DeepLinking>` component can be included anywhere in the application:

```
export class RootComponent extends Component {
    render() {
        return (
            <View style={styles.container}>
                <DeepLinking />
                <View style={styles.nav}>
                    <Link to="/app.chapter7.com">
                        <Text>Home</Text>
                    </Link>
                    <Link to="/app.chapter7.com/dashboard">
                        <Text>Dashboard</Text>
                    </Link>
                </View>
                <View style={styles.routeContainer}>
                    <Route path="/app.chapter7.com" exact component={HomeComponent} />
                    <Route path="/app.chapter7.com/dashboard" component={DashboardComponent} />
                </View>
            </View>
        )
    }
}
```

Here, the `<DeepLinking>` component is included in the `RootComponent` of the application, and also the `<Route>` paths are updated with the prefix `app.chapter7.com` to match the hostname declared in the `AndroidManifest.xml` file.

To test deep-linking, try the following command:

```
adb shell am start -W -a android.intent.action.VIEW -d deeplink://app.chapter7.com/dashboard
```

The previous command should launch the application on the AVD and navigate you to the route with the `/dashboard` path.

Summary

In this chapter, we looked at how React Router's `<NativeRouter>` component can be used in a React Native application. The `<NativeRouter>` component is available in the `react-router-native` package, and it uses the `<MemoryRouter>` component internally, which is defined in the `react-router` package. The `<NativeRouter>` component accepts props: `initialEntries`, `initialIndex`, `getUserConfirmation`, `keyLength`, and `children`. Also, it provides a default implementation for the `getUserConfirmation` function, which uses React Native's `Alert` component to display a confirmation message. This confirmation message is shown when the `<Prompt>` component is included in the application and the user tries to navigate away from the current route.

The `<BackButton>` component in `react-router-native` is a wrapper around React Native's `BackHandler` class, which listens to the devices' back button and navigates the user back by one entry in the history stack. The `<DeepLinking>` component is used to handle deep links to the content in the application. The component uses React Native's `Linking` interface to listen to the URL changes and it navigates the user to the requested route when the application is accessed using a deep link URI scheme. To define a URI scheme for the application, the `AndroidManifest.xml` manifest file is updated with `<intent-filter>` for the main activity (`.MainActivity`). `intent-filter` declares the URI scheme and the hostname to use to access the content inside the application.

In the next chapter, we will take a look at the state management tool, Redux, and understand how React Router can be used in conjunction with Redux.

8
Redux Bindings with connected-react-router

In previous chapters, we looked at how the component's state can be used to store model data and how React updates the view when the model is updated as a result of a user action. In large applications, this state information should be made available not only to the current component and its children but also to other components in the application tree. There are various state management libraries available that aid in keeping the user interface components in sync with the application state. Redux is one such library that uses a central data store to manage the state of the application. The store serves as a source of truth and the components in the application can rely on the state maintained in the store.

In this chapter, we will take a look at the `connected-react-router` library, which provides Redux bindings for React Router. The following topics are discussed in this chapter:

- State management with Redux—An introduction to Redux concepts
- Getting started with `connected-react-router`
- Reading the react-router state from the Redux store
- Navigating to different routes by dispatching actions

State management with Redux

As mentioned, Redux uses a single store to manage the state of the application. Apart from `Store`, there are two other building blocks: `Actions` and `Reducers`.

Let's take a look at how these building blocks help maintain `state` and update the view when `state` in `Store` changes.

Actions

Actions let you define the operations that the user can perform to update the state of the application. An Action is a JavaScript object of the `{ type, payload }` shape, where `type` is a string mentioning the user action and `payload` is the data with which the state should be updated:

```
let todoId = 0;
export const addTodo = text => ({
    type: 'ADD_TODO'
    payload: {
        text,
        id: todoId++,
        isCompleted: false
    }
})
```

Here, the `addTodo` action accepts a TODO text and indicates that the Action is used to add a TODO to a list of TODOs. `payload` here is an object containing the TODO `text`, a TODO ID, and a Boolean flag, `isCompleted` (set to false). It's also possible to have actions that don't require the `payload` property to be included. For example, consider the following action:

```
export const increment = () => ({
    type: 'INCREMENT'
})
```

Here, the `action` type `INCREMENT` indicates that the value of an entity has to be incremented by one. The preceding `action` does not need a `payload` property and based on the action type, the state of the entity can be updated.

Reducers

A Reducer in Redux alters the state of an entity based on the action dispatched to the store. A Reducer is a pure function that accepts two parameters: state and action. The Reducer then returns an updated state based on the value store in action.type. For example, consider the following reducer:

```
const todoReducer = (state = [], action) => {
    switch (action.type) {
        case 'ADD_TODO':
            return [
                ...state,
                {
                    id: action.payload.id,
                    text: action.payload.text,
                    isCompleted: action.payload.isCompleted
                }
            ];
        default:
            return state;
    }
}
```

The initial state of todoReducer is set to an empty array (state parameter's default value) and a TODO is added to the list when the action type is ADD_TODO. One of the core tenets of Redux is not to mutate the state tree, but rather return a new state tree as a result of an action dispatched by the component. This helps to keep the reducer function pure (that is, with no side effects), and helps in recognizing the new state change when the React component re-renders the view elements.

Similarly, there could be multiple actions that update the TODO state (such as MARK_COMPLETED and DELETE), and the reducer can alter the state of the TODO list based on the action type dispatched to the store.

Store

Store is a central data object from which the application state can be derived. The components in the application subscribe to the changes in the store's state and update the view.

Here's how the data flows in Redux:

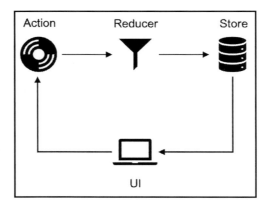

The user performs an operation, such as submitting a form or clicking a button, thus dispatching an action to the store. The application defines various actions that the user can perform and reducer is coded so that it can handle these actions and update the state of the entity. The state of various entities in the application is maintained in one central location: the store. For example, the application could have various entities, such as Todo and the User profile, and the store would maintain the state information for these entities. Whenever the reducer updates the state value of a particular entity in the store, the user interface component receives an update from the store, updating the component's state information and re-rendering the view with the updated state.

Redux in React

After creating a project using the `create-react-app` CLI, include the dependencies `redux` and `react-redux` dependencies:

```
npm install --save redux react-redux
```

The `redux` library includes the `createStore`, `combineReducers`, `bindActionCreators`, `applyMiddleware`, and `compose` helper functions; whereas the `react-redux` library includes Redux bindings that help your React components communicate with the Redux store.

The next step is to define actions that the user can initiate from the user interface. In our example, we will create a `Counter` component that can `increment` and `decrement` the counter value.

In `actions/counter.js`:

```
export const increment = () => ({
    type: 'INCREMENT'
});

export const decrement = () => ({
    type: 'DECREMENT'
});
```

After defining actions for our counter entity, the `reducer` that updates the state of the `counter` needs to be defined:

In `reducers/counter.js`:

```
const counterReducer = (state = 0, action) => {
    switch (action.type) {
        case 'INCREMENT':
            return state + 1;
        case 'DECREMENT':
            return state - 1;
        default:
            return state;
    }
}

export default counterReducer;
```

The `reducer` defined here updates the `state` value based on the type of `action` triggered by the user. Similarly, you can have various reducers and actions in the application that update the entity's state when a certain action is triggered by the user.

The `combineReducers` utility from `redux` allows you to combine all the reducers into one single reducer, which can then be used in `initializing` the store for the application.

In `reducers/index.js`:

```
import { combineReducers } from 'redux';
import counterReducer from './counter';

const rootReducer = combineReducers({
    count: counterReducer,
    todo: todoReducer
});

export default rootReducer;
```

Redux Bindings with connected-react-router

A `rootReducer` is created using the `combineReducers` function, which accepts an object with a key-value mapping of an entity and a reducer. Here `counterReducer` is assigned to the `count` entity and `todoReducer` is assigned to an entity with the `todo` key.

`rootReducer` is then used in the `createStore` function to create a store.

In `index.js`:

```
import { createStore } from 'redux';

const store = createStore(
    rootReducer
);
```

The store is made available to the components in the application using the `<Provider>` component defined in the `react-redux` library:

```
ReactDOM.render(
    <Provider store={store}>
        <Counter />
    </Provider>,
    document.getElementById('root')
);
```

The components in the application can now subscribe to the state changes in the entities (`count` and `todo`) in the store using the `connect` higher-order function. A `Counter` component is created, which will display the current state value of `count` and will dispatch the `increment` and `decrement` actions that we defined in `actions/counter.js`.

In `components/counter.component.js`:

```
import { increment, decrement } from '../actions/counter';
const Counter = ({ count, increment, decrement }) => (
    <div>
        <h4>Counter</h4>
        <button onClick={decrement}>-</button>
        <span>{count}</span>
        <button onClick={increment}>+</button>
    </div>
)
```

The `count`, `increment`, and `decrement` props are made available from the `store` using the following `connect` method:

```
import { connect } from 'react-redux';
import { increment, decrement } from '../actions/counter';

...

const mapStateToProps = state => ({
    count: state.count
});

const mapDispatchToProps = dispatch => ({
    increment: () => dispatch(increment()),
    decrement: () => dispatch(decrement())
})

export default connect(mapStateToProps, mapDispatchToProps)(Counter);
```

The `connect` higher-order function from `react-redux` helps you to inject the Redux state into your React components. The `connect` HOC accepts two arguments: `mapStateToProps` and `mapDispathToProps`. As observed, the Redux state `count` property is assigned to the component's state `count` property in `mapStateToProps`, and similarly, the component can dispatch actions to the store using the `increment` and `decrement` actions specified in `mapDispatchToProps`. Here, to read the state values from the Redux store, `mapStateToProps` is used, and `connect` provides the entire state tree to the component so that the component can read from various objects in the state tree. To alter the state of the tree, `mapDispatchToProps` helps in dispatching actions registered with the store. The `connect` HOC provides the `dispatch` method so that the component can invoke actions on the store.

Getting started with connected-react-router

The `connected-react-router` library provides Redux bindings for React Router; for example, the application's history can be read from a Redux store and you can navigate to different routes in the application by dispatching actions to the store.

Let's first install `connected-react-router` and other libraries using `npm`:

```
npm install --save connected-react-router  react-router  react-router-dom history
```

Redux Bindings with connected-react-router

Next, we will update the store settings.

In `index.js`:

```
import { applyMiddleware, createStore, compose } from 'redux';
import { ConnectedRouter, connectRouter, routerMiddleware } from
'connected-react-router';

const history = createBrowserHistory();

const composeEnhancer = window.__REDUX_DEVTOOLS_EXTENSION_COMPOSE__ ||
compose;

const store = createStore(
    connectRouter(history)(rootReducer),
    composeEnhancer(applyMiddleware(routerMiddleware(history)))
);
```

The `createStore` function has the following signature:

```
createStore(reducer, preloadedState, enhancer)
```

It accepts three parameters: the first parameter is the `reducer` function, which returns the next state tree given the current state tree and the action to handle; the second parameter specifies the initial `state` of the application and should be an object with the same shape as the one used in `combineReducers`; the third parameter specifies the store `enhancer`, which adds more capabilities to the store, such as time travel, persistence, and so on.

In our example, the first parameter is as follows:

```
connectRouter(history)(rootReducer)
```

`connectRouter` from `connected-react-router` wraps `rootReducer` and returns a new root reducer with the `router` state in it. The `connectRouter` reducer responds to actions with type `@@router/LOCATION_CHANGE` to update the router state. Notice that `connectRouter` accepts the `history` object as its parameter; `connectRouter` then uses the history object to initialize the router state with the `location` and `action` properties.

The second parameter to `createStore` is enhancer:

```
composeEnhancer = window.__REDUX_DEVTOOLS_EXTENSION_COMPOSE__ || compose;
...
composeEnhancer(applyMiddleware(routerMiddleware(history)))
```

Please note that we're specifying `enhancer` as the second parameter. The `createStore` method marks the second parameter as `enhancer` if it is a function and when the third parameter to `createStore` is not specified. The `compose` utility in `redux` returns a function obtained by composing given functions from right to left. In the previous case, we are checking whether the `Redux Devtools Extension` is available in the browser, which enables you to view the state of various entities in the application.

`routerMiddleware` defined in `connected-react-router` is a middleware function used to redirect the user using the provided `history` object. If an action of the `'CALL_HISTORY_METHOD'` type is dispatched, the middleware function will navigate the user to the requested route by calling one of the methods on the `history` object. It also prevents the action (`CALL_HISTORY_METHOD`) from reaching other reducers defined in the application and the middleware components that are defined after `routerMiddleware`.

The `applyMiddleware` utility in Redux is used to create a store enhancer, which applies middleware to the dispatch method of the Redux store.

The next step is to make the store (created with `createStore`) available to the components in the application using the `<Provider>` component:

```
ReactDOM.render(
    <Provider store={store}>
        <ConnectedRouter history={history}>
            <App />
        </ConnectedRouter>
    </Provider>,
document.getElementById('root'));
```

Here, we have wrapped the application root component inside the `<ConnectedRouter>` component, which, in turn, is wrapped inside the `<Provider>` component. This is required since `ConnectedRouter` subscribes to the changes in the `router` state to see whether the `location` property has changed and then calls the `history.push` method to navigate the user to the requested route.

With these changes, the components in our application can now read the state information from the store and also dispatch actions to navigate to various routes defined in the application.

Reading state information from the Redux store

To test the preceding setup, let's first create a `<Link>` component in our navbar and a corresponding `<Route>` with the same path name:

```
<Link
    to={{
        pathname: '/dashboard',
        search: 'q=1',
        hash: 'test',
        state: { key: 'value' }
    }}
>
    Dashboard
</Link>
...
<Route path='/dashboard' component={Dashboard} />
```

Notice that the `<Link>` component specifies the `to` object with the `pathname`, `search`, `hash`, and `state` properties. We will read this information from the Redux store in our rendered component:

```
const Dashboard = ({ pathname, search, hash, state, count }) => {
    return (
        <div>
            <h4>In Dashboard</h4>
            <div> Pathname   : {pathname} </div>
            <div> Search     : {search} </div>
            <div> Hash       : {hash} </div>
            <div> State-Key  : {state? state.key : null} </div>
        </div>
    )
}

const mapStateToProps = state => ({
    pathname: state.router.location.pathname,
    search: state.router.location.search,
    hash: state.router.location.hash,
    state: state.router.location.state
});

export default connect(mapStateToProps)(Dashboard);
```

From this code snippet, the `pathname`, `search`, `location`, and `hash` properties are read from `state.router.location`. As mentioned earlier, the `connectRouter` function creates the `router` state and it updates the value when an action of type `LOCATION_CHANGE` has been dispatched. The `<ConnectRouter>` component listens to the changes in the history object and then dispatches the `LOCATION_CHANGE` action whenever you try to navigate using the `<Link>` component.

If you have Redux Dev Tools installed in Chrome (available in the Chrome Web Store), you can observe the action dispatched when you try to navigate from one route to the other:

In this **Dev Tools** window, the `@@router/LOCATION_CHANGE` action is dispatched when you try to navigate, and the action in the following section shows the payload provided when dispatching the action.

Navigating by dispatching actions

The `connected-react-router` library provides actions that you can dispatch from your components to navigate to the routes defined in the application. These include `push`, `replace`, `go`, `goBack`, and `goForward`. These methods call the corresponding methods on the history object to navigate to the specified path.

The `DashboardComponent` in the previous example can now be updated to use `mapDispatchToProps`:

```
import {push, replace} from 'connected-react-router';

const Dashboard = ({ pathname, search, hash, state, count, push, replace }) => {
    return (
        ...
<button onClick={() => {push('/')}}>HOME</button>
        <button onClick={() => {replace('/counter')}}>COUNTER</button>
        ...
    )
}

const mapStateToProps = state => ({
...
});

const mapDispatchToProps = dispatch => ({
    push: (path) => dispatch(push(path)),
    replace: (path) => dispatch(replace(path))
});

export default connect(mapStateToProps, mapDispatchToProps)(Dashboard);
```

The preceding component now dispatches `push` and `replace` actions when you click on the **HOME** and the **COUNTER** buttons respectively. The `mapDispatchToProps` function enables you to dispatch actions to the store and, in our example, the `push` and `replace` functions accept a `pathname` to dispatch actions.

Summary

In this chapter, we looked at how the Redux library can be used to create a store to manage various state entities in the application. The store receives actions and the reducers alter the state of the application when an action is dispatched. The `connected-react-router` library provides Redux bindings for React Router and it includes a higher-order function, `connectRouter`, which wraps `rootReducer` and creates a `router` state. The `connectRouter` function is then used in the `createStore` function to make the `router` state available to the components in the application.

The `<ConnectedRouter>` component in `connected-react-router` listens to the changes in the `history` location and dispatches the `LOCATION_CHANGE` action to update the `router` state property. This `router` state property can then be read by the rendered route component by reading the state information from the store.

The library also includes the `push`, `replace`, `go`, `goBack`, and `goForward` actions, which the component can dispatch to navigate to the routes defined in the application.

Other Books You May Enjoy

If you enjoyed this book, you may be interested in these other books by Packt:

React Design Patterns and Best Practices
Michele Bertoli

ISBN: 978-1-78646-453-8

- Write clean and maintainable code
- Create reusable components applying consolidated techniques
- Use React effectively in the browser and node
- Choose the right styling approach according to the needs of the applications
- Use server-side rendering to make applications load faster
- Build high-performing applications by optimizing components

React Cookbook
Carlos Santana Roldan

ISBN: 978-1-78398-072-7

- Gain the ability to wield complex topics such as Webpack and server-side rendering
- Implement an API using Node.js, Firebase, and GraphQL
- Learn to maximize the performance of React applications
- Create a mobile application using React Native
- Deploy a React application on Digital Ocean
- Get to know the best practices when organizing and testing a large React application

Leave a review - let other readers know what you think

Please share your thoughts on this book with others by leaving a review on the site that you bought it from. If you purchased the book from Amazon, please leave us an honest review on this book's Amazon page. This is vital so that other potential readers can see and use your unbiased opinion to make purchasing decisions, we can understand what our customers think about our products, and our authors can see your feedback on the title that they have worked with Packt to create. It will only take a few minutes of your time, but is valuable to other potential customers, our authors, and Packt. Thank you!

Index

A

actions
  dispatching, for navigation 136
application routes
  defining 17, 19
authorization
  managing 61, 62, 63

B

BackButton component 117
bookmarkable URLs 13
BrowserRouter component
  about 78
  basename prop 79
  custom dialog box, displaying with
    getUserConfirmation prop 82, 85
  forceRefresh prop 80
  getUserConfirmation prop 81
  keyLength prop 80, 81

C

callback route
  redirecting with 63, 64, 65
connected-react-router
  about 131
  implementing 132, 133
  installing 131
create-react-native-app CLI
  ejecting from 119
  project, creating 108, 110
custom dialog box
  displaying, with getUserConfirmation prop 83, 85

D

DeepLinking component
  create-react-native-app, ejecting 119
  including 122, 123
  intent-filter, adding to manifest file 120
Deeplinks
  creating, with DeepLinking component 118
dynamic routes
  from JSON 37, 39
dynamic routing 34, 36, 37

E

Express.js
  about 90
  used, for Server-Side Rendering (SSR) of React application 90

G

getUserConfirmation prop
  custom dialog box, displaying 83, 85

H

hashbang
  reference 88
HashRouter component
  about 86, 87
  hashType prop 87
history object
  about 29
  action property 29
  block() function 29
  createHref() function 30
  go(n) function 30
  goBack() function 30
  goForward() function 30
  length property 29
  listen(listenerFn) function 30
  location property 29
  push(path, state?) function 30

replace(path, state?) function 30
history
    route, navigating programmatically 50

I

Isomorphic React applications
    creating 102, 103
    Server-Side configuration 105
    webpack, configuration 104, 105

J

JSON
    dynamic routes 37, 39
JSX 8

L

Link component
    about 42
    innerRef prop 43
    replace prop 43
    to prop, with object 44, 45
location object 30

M

match object 31

N

NativeRouter component
    adding 110, 111, 113, 114
    implementing 115
    initialEntries prop 116
    initialIndex prop 116, 117
    project, creating with create-react-native-app CLI 108, 110
    using, in React Native application 108
navigation
    actions, dispatching 136
navigational components 13
NavLink component
    about 46
    activeClassName prop 46
    activeStyle prop 47
    exact prop 47
    isActive prop 48

location prop 49
strict prop 48
nested routes
    about 34, 36, 37
    navigating to 50
Node.js
    about 90
    used, for Server-Side Rendering (SSR) of React application 90

O

one-way data binding 9

P

Prompt
    transitions, preventing 53, 54

R

React component
    creating 10
React Native 13
React Router, packages
    react-router 13
    react-router-dom 13
    react-router-native 13
React Router
    about 12
    adding 16
    application routes, defining 17, 19
    features 13
    implementing 14, 15
React
    about 7
    component-based architecture 9
    features 8
    overview 8
Redirect component
    about 58
    push prop 60
    to prop 58, 60
    used, for redirecting to Page Not Found page 69
    using, in Switch component 69
Redux store
    state information, reading 134, 135, 136
Redux

in React 128, 130, 131
state management 126
Route component props
    about 29
    history object 29, 30
    location object 30
    match object 31, 32
Route component
    using, in Switch component 66
    with path '/' as first child, in Switch component 66
    with path params, in Switch component 67
Route parameters 32
Route props
    about 24
    exact prop 24, 25
    inline rendering, with children prop 28
    inline rendering, with render prop 27
    sensitive prop 26
    strict prop 25
Router component
    about 74
    including, from react-router package 75, 76
    react-router package 76
    react-router-dom package 77
routes
    navigating to, programmatically with history 50
    protecting 61, 62, 63
    redirecting, with callback route 63, 64, 65

S

Server-Side Rendering (SSR)
    about 89
    dependencies, installing 90
    of React application, with Express.js 90
    of React application, with Node.js 90
    React application, rendering with
      ReactDOMServer.renderToString 93
    Server-Side application, starting 92
    webpack, build configuration 91
single page applications (SPAs) 7

state information
    reading, from Redux store 134, 135, 136
state management
    actions 126
    with Reducers 127
    with Redux 126
    with Store 127
StaticRouter component
    adding 94
    context prop 100
    Redirect component, used for Server-Side
      redirect 96, 97
    requested URL, matching with matchPath 98
    routes, creating 94
    staticContext, used for Server-Side redirect 96, 97
Switch component
    404 – Page Not Found, adding 67, 69
    exclusive routing 65
    Redirect component, using 69
    redirecting, to new path 70
    Route components, ordering 66

T

transitions
    preventing, with Prompt 53, 54

V

virtual DOM 9

W

webpack
    about 91
    configuration 91
withRouter
    using 51, 52, 53

Y

yarn package manager
    reference 15

Made in the USA
Columbia, SC
06 June 2021